CAMBRIDGE
Primary Science

Learner's Book 4

Fiona Baxter & Liz Dilley

CAMBRIDGE
UNIVERSITY PRESS

University Printing House, Cambridge CB2 8BS, United Kingdom

One Liberty Plaza, 20th Floor, New York, NY 10006, USA

477 Williamstown Road, Port Melbourne, VIC 3207, Australia

314–321, 3rd Floor, Plot 3, Splendor Forum, Jasola District Centre, New Delhi – 110025, India

103 Penang Road, #05-06/07, Visioncrest Commercial, Singapore 238467

Cambridge University Press is part of the University of Cambridge.

It furthers the University's mission by disseminating knowledge in the pursuit of education, learning and research at the highest international levels of excellence.

www.cambridge.org
Information on this title: www.cambridge.org/9781108742931

© Cambridge University Press 2021

This publication is in copyright. Subject to statutory exception and to the provisions of relevant collective licensing agreements, no reproduction of any part may take place without the written permission of Cambridge University Press.

First published 2014

Second edition 2021

20 19

Printed in Italy by L.E.G.O. S.p.A.

A catalogue record for this publication is available from the British Library

978-1-108-74293-1 Paperback with Digital Access (1 Year)

978-1-108-97260-4 Digital Learner's Book (1 Year)

978-1-108-97259-8 eBook

Cambridge University Press has no responsibility for the persistence or accuracy of URLs for external or third-party internet websites referred to in this publication, and does not guarantee that any content on such websites is, or will remain, accurate or appropriate. Information regarding prices, travel timetables, and other factual information given in this work is correct at the time of first printing but Cambridge University Press does not guarantee the accuracy of such information thereafter.

Cambridge International copyright material in this publication is reproduced under licence and remains the intellectual property of Cambridge Assessment International Education.

NOTICE TO TEACHERS IN THE UK
It is illegal to reproduce any part of this work in material form (including photocopying and electronic storage) except under the following circumstances:
(i)   where you are abiding by a licence granted to your school or institution by the Copyright Licensing Agency;
(ii) where no such licence exists, or where you wish to exceed the terms of a licence, and you have gained the written permission of Cambridge University Press;
(iii) where you are allowed to reproduce without permission under the provisions of Chapter 3 of the Copyright, Designs and Patents Act 1988, which covers, for example, the reproduction of short passages within certain types of educational anthology and reproduction for the purposes of setting examination questions.

Introduction

Welcome to Stage 4 of Cambridge Primary Science. We hope this book will show you how interesting and exciting Science can be.

People have always asked questions about things they observed and looked for answers to their questions. Have you ever wondered about any of these questions?

- How do our muscles work?
- Why can we see ourselves in a mirror?
- Why do liquids freeze and solids melt?
- Why do we have day and night?
- Why do volcanoes erupt?
- Why does a lamp light up when you switch it on?

You will work like a scientist to find the answers to some of these questions. You will also ask your own questions to investigate.

You will be able to practise new skills and check how you are doing and also challenge yourself to find out more. We have included a variety of different activities and exercises for you to try.

We use science in our lives every day. You will learn about some of the things that scientists in the past discovered and invented. You will also find out how some people around you use science and how using science can help or harm our environment.

We hope you enjoy thinking and working like a scientist.

Fiona Baxter and Liz Dilley

Contents

Page	Unit	Science strand	Thinking and Working Scientifically strand	Science in Context
viii	Working like a scientist			
2 2 6 9 15 22	1 Living things 1.1 Bones and skeletons 1.2 Why we need a skeleton 1.3 Skeletons and movement 1.4 Different kinds of skeletons 1.5 Medicines and infectious diseases	Biology: Structure and function Biology: Life processes	Models and representations Scientific enquiry: purpose and planning Carrying out scientific enquiry Scientific enquiry: analysis, evaluation and conclusions	Describe how science is used where you live. Discuss how science positively and negatively affects the environment where you live.
31 31 35 39 43	2 Energy 2.1 Energy around us 2.2 Energy transfers 2.3 Energy changes 2.4 Energy and living things	Physics: Forces and energy Biology: Life processes Biology: Ecosystems	Models and representations Scientific enquiry: purpose and planning Carrying out scientific enquiry	Describe how science is used where you live. Discuss how science positively and negatively affects the environment where you live.
49 49 54 58 63	3 Materials 3.1 Materials, substances and particles 3.2 How do solids and liquids behave? 3.3 Melting and solidifying 3.4 Chemical reactions	Chemistry: Materials and their structure Chemistry: Properties of materials Chemistry: Changes to materials	Models and representations Scientific enquiry: purpose and planning Carrying out scientific enquiry Scientific enquiry: analysis, evaluation and conclusions	Describe how science is used where you live.

Contents

Page	Unit	Science strand	Thinking and Working Scientifically strand	Science in Context
70 70 75 82 87	**4 Earth and its habitats** 4.1 The structure of the Earth 4.2 Volcanoes 4.3 Earthquakes 4.4 Different habitats	Earth and Space: Planet Earth Biology: Ecosystems	Models and representations Carrying out scientific enquiry Scientific enquiry: analysis, evaluation and conclusions	Find out who uses science where you live and how they use it.
96 96 99 103 108 113 116	**5 Light** 5.1 How we see things 5.2 Light travels in straight lines 5.3 Light reflects off different surfaces 5.4 Light in the solar system 5.5 Day and night 5.6 Investigating shadow lengths	Physics: Light and sound Earth and Space: Earth in space	Scientific enquiry: purpose and planning Carrying out scientific enquiry	Use evidence to show how our scientific knowledge and understanding have changed over time. Use science in discussions to support your ideas.
124 124 128 132 137 140	**6 Electricity** 6.1 Which materials conduct electricity? 6.2 Does water conduct electricity? 6.3 Using conductors and insulators in electrical appliances 6.4 Switches 6.5 Changing the number of components in a circuit	Physics: Electricity and magnetism	Scientific enquiry: purpose and planning	Use evidence to show how our scientific knowledge and understanding have changed over time.
148 154 163	**New science skills** **Glossary and index** **Acknowledgements**			

v

How to use this book

In this book you will find lots of different features to help your learning

What you will learn in the topic →

> **We are going to...**
> - name some of the bones in our body
> - point out where some of the main bones are found in our body
> - make a model of a skeleton
> - think about how a model is different to the real thing.

Questions to find out what you know already →

> **Getting started**
>
> The picture shows a skeleton.
> 1. What is a skeleton?
> 2. What is the skeleton made of?
> 3. What type of animal do you think the skeleton comes from?
> 4. Name the parts of the animal's body you can see in its skeleton.

Important words to learn →

> bones   rib cage
> frame   skeleton
> hip   skull
> jaw   spine
> model

> **Activity**
>
> **Summarise the structure of the Earth**
>
> Copy the table. Some information is filled in already. Use information from the diagram and information about the structure of the Earth to complete the table.
>
> | Name of layer | Crust | | |
> |---|---|---|---|
> | Thickness | | 3000 km | |
> | Material | | | Iron and nickel |
> | Temperature | | | 5000 – 6000 °C |
> | Solid or liquid? | Solid | | |
>
> **How am I doing?**
> Exchange your completed table with a partner. Check any differences with your teacher.

A fun activity about the science you are learning →

> **Think like a scientist**
>
> **Make a model skeleton**
>
> A model helps us understand how something works or see what something looks like that we cannot see in real life. Work with a partner to make a model of a skeleton.
>
> **You will need:**
> drinking straws and bottle tops, modelling clay or different shapes of pasta, scissors, black construction paper or stiff card, paper glue, white paper, a pen
>
> - Look at the picture of the human skeleton.
>   Notice the sizes and shapes of the bones and how they are arranged.
> - Plan how you will make a skeleton from drinking straws and modelling clay or different pasta shapes. Your skeleton should show these bones: skull, jaw, rib cage, spine, arm bones and leg bones.
> - Arrange the parts of your model on the paper to make the skeleton.
> - When you are happy with your skeleton, glue the parts onto the paper.
> - Write labels for the different bones of your skeleton.
>   Stick the labels on the paper next to the bones they name.

An investigation to carry out with a partner or in groups →

vi

How to use this book

Questions to help you think about how you learn ──▶

> What did you learn about skeletons?
> What did you find difficult?
> What did you find fun to learn?

This is what you have learned in the topic ──▶

Look what I can do!
- ☐ I can describe the main functions of the skeleton as protecting organs, allowing movement, giving shape to the body and supporting organs during activity.
- ☐ I can understand that we grow because our skeleton grows.
- ☐ I can measure the length of bones.
- ☐ I can record data in a table.

At the end of each unit, there is a project for you to carry out, using what you have learned. You might make something or solve a problem ──▶

Project: Earthworm farming

Earthworms are invertebrates. Earthworms live in the earth or soil.

People all over the world keep earthworm farms. They grow the earthworms in containers that are dark and moist inside, like the soil.

The farmers feed the worms with materials such as vegetable peels and garden waste. Earthworms leave droppings called 'castings'. The earthworms' castings form a substance called worm compost. The worm compost contain substances that help plants to grow better. The worm farmers sell the worm compost to gardeners and other farmers.

Questions
Work in pairs.
Speak to someone in your local area who farms earthworms.
These are some questions you could ask:

Questions that cover what you have learned in the unit. If you can answer these, you are ready to move onto the next unit ──▶

Check your progress
1. Write the word that describes each of the following:
   a. A frame made of bone that supports our body.
   b. The bones of the head.
   c. Something that shows us how another thing looks or works.
   d. The parts inside our bodies.
   e. Animals with no backbone.
   f. The parts of the body that allow our bones to move.
   g. The hard skin or shell on the outside of the body of some animals.
   h. An injection that prevents disease.
2. Look at the drawing and answer the questions.
   a. Write down the number of the muscle that bends the arm.
   b. Underline the correct words in the sentences to explain how the muscle makes the arm bend upwards.

   The muscle **contracts/relaxes**. The muscles gets **longer/shorter** and **pushes/pulls** on the arm bone.

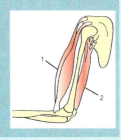

vii

Working like a scientist

Scientists ask questions about the world around them. They then try to find answers to the questions. Scientists use different types of scientific enquiry to help them find the answers. Young scientists, like you, can do the same to find answers to scientific questions.

Research

We can speak to people, or use books and the internet, to find information to answer questions such as:

- How did vaccinations first start?
- What are earthquakes and why do they happen?

Fair testing

We carry out fair tests to find out how changing one thing in an investigation makes another thing change. The things that we change, keep the same and measure are called variables. We can use a fair test to answer questions such as:

- Does the type of material affect how well heat energy is transferred?
- Does changing the number of cells in a circuit make a lamp brighter or dimmer?

Working like a scientist

Observing over time

We sometimes need to observe living things, materials or processes over time to find out how they change. For example:

- How does ice change when we heat it?
- How do shadows change during the day?

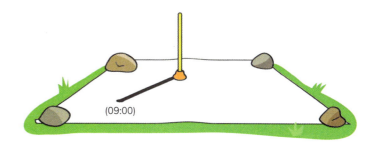

Identifying and classifying

We make observations and measurements to help us look for similarities and differences in objects, materials and living things. This helps us to organise things into groups. For example:

- How can we group animals based on what they eat?
- Which materials conduct electricity?

Pattern seeking

In this type of scientific enquiry, we try to answer questions by identifying patterns in the measurements and observations we record. For example:

- Is there a pattern between the size and shape of a bird's beak and the food it will eat?
- Does particle size change how fast a powder solid flows?

1 Living Things

> 1.1 Bones and skeletons

We are going to...

- name some of the bones in our body
- point out where some of the main bones are found in our body
- make a model of a skeleton
- think about how a model is different to the real thing.

bones | rib cage
frame | skeleton
hip | skull
jaw | spine
model

Getting started

The picture shows a skeleton.

1. What is a skeleton?
2. What is the skeleton made of?
3. What type of animal do you think the skeleton comes from?
4. Name the parts of the animal's body you can see in its skeleton.

1.1 Bones and skeletons

What is a skeleton?

People and many animals have **bones** inside their bodies. These bones are joined together to form a skeleton. A skeleton is a strong **frame** that supports our body from the inside.

We know about animals, like dinosaurs, that lived very long ago from their skeletons.

The human skeleton

Our skeletons are made of 206 bones. These bones are different sizes and shapes.

You can feel your bones through your skin. Bones are hard and strong. How many bones in your body can you name?

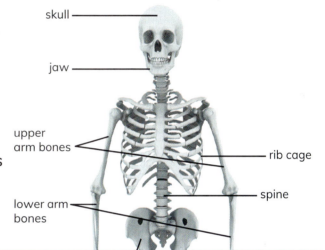

Activity

Finding your bones

- Feel your head. How many **skull** bones can you feel?
- Push a finger on your chin and feel the bone. Your chin is part of your **jaw** bone.
- Hold your hands on the sides of your chest. Can you find your **rib cage**?
- How many ribs can you feel?
- Now feel your back. The bumps you can feel are the bones of your **spine**.
- Stand up and put your hands on your **hips**. Can you feel your hip bones?

3

1 Living Things

Continued

- Find your arm bones. Can you feel how many there are?
- Feel your leg bones. Is the bone in your upper leg (thigh bone) the same size as the bones in your lower leg?
- Point out the bones you have found to a partner. Name the bones.

Questions

1 What are skeletons made of?
2 Why must skeletons be hard and strong?
3 Why do you think the bones of your skeleton are different sizes and shapes?
4 Bones are not very heavy. How do you think this helps animals?

Think like a scientist

Make a model skeleton

A **model** helps us understand how something works or see what something looks like that we cannot see in real life. Work with a partner to make a model of a skeleton.

> **You will need:**
> drinking straws and bottle tops, modelling clay or different shapes of pasta, scissors, black construction paper or stiff card, paper glue, white paper, a pen

- Look at the picture of the human skeleton.
  Notice the sizes and shapes of the bones and how they are arranged.
- Plan how you will make a skeleton from drinking straws and modelling clay or different pasta shapes. Your skeleton should show these bones: skull, jaw, rib cage, spine, arm bones and leg bones.
- Arrange the parts of your model on the paper to make the skeleton.
- When you are happy with your skeleton, glue the parts onto the paper.
- Write labels for the different bones of your skeleton.
  Stick the labels on the paper next to the bones they name.

1.1 Bones and skeletons

> **Continued**
>
> **Questions**
>
> 1. How is your model of a skeleton the same as a real skeleton? How is it different?
> 2. Look at other pairs' models. Can you think of any ways you could make your model better?

What did you learn about skeletons?
What did you find difficult?
What did you find fun to learn?

> **Look what I can do!**
>
> ☐ I can identify the skull, jaw, spine, rib cage, arm bones and leg bones in my body.
> ☐ I can make a model of a skeleton.
> ☐ I can explain how a model is different to the real thing.

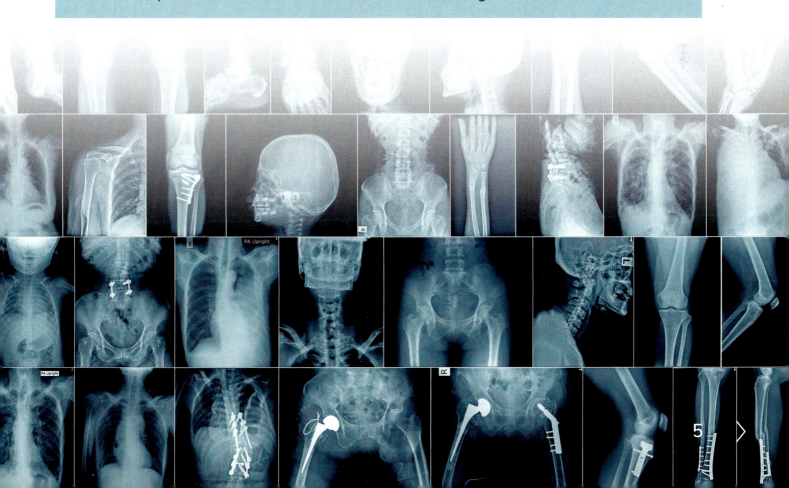

1 Living Things

> 1.2 Why we need a skeleton

We are going to...
- describe the main functions of the skeleton
- measure the length of bones
- think about why it is better to measure in standard units
- record data in a table.

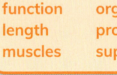

function   organs
length   protect
muscles   support

Getting started

1 What is the role of the skeleton?
2 Think of some reasons why we need a skeleton.
3 Name any of the parts inside your body that you know of.

Our skeleton has four main jobs or **functions**.

Skeletons protect

The parts inside our bodies are called **organs**. The body organs do important jobs that keep us alive and healthy. Our skeletons **protect** the main organs of our bodies.

Skeletons give shape

The bones of our skeleton are strong. The skeleton forms a frame that **supports** or holds up the rest of the body and gives the body its shape. Our skeleton makes our body firm. We cannot squash our body easily because we have skeleton.

Skeletons allow us to move

Our skeleton helps us to walk, run and move in lots of different ways. We can move because there are **muscles** joined to bones of the skeleton. Muscles are parts of the body that help us to move.

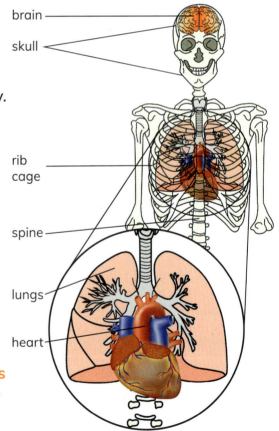

1.2 Why we need a skeleton

Questions

1. **How** does the skeleton protect the brain?
2. Which organs does the rib cage protect?
3. Why do we need strong bones?
4. Explain how our skeleton helps us to move.

Skeletons help us grow

We grow and get bigger because our skeleton grows. An adult's skeleton is much bigger than a child's skeleton. An adult's skeleton has stopped growing.

Think like a scientist

Measuring bone lengths

Work with a partner.

You will need: a tape measure

Use the tape measure to measure the **length**, from end to end, of each other's:

- upper arm bone
- upper leg bone
- lower leg bone.

Record the measurements in a table like the one shown here.

Bone	Length in cm	
	Me	Partner
Upper arm bone		
Lower arm bone		
Lower leg bone		

1. Whose bones are longer?
2. Predict what you think the length of a teenager's bones would be. Say why.
3. Marcus and Arun did not have a measuring tape to do their investigation. They counted how many hand lengths long their bones were. Is this a good method to measure bone length? Say why or why not.

1 Living Things

> **Continued**
>
> **How am I doing?**
>
> Answer 'Very well', 'Quite well' or 'I need help' to these questions:
> - How well can I measure the length of bones?
> - How well can I record data in a table?

> **Look what I can do!**
>
> ☐ I can describe the main functions of the skeleton as protecting organs, allowing movement, giving shape to the body and supporting organs during activity.
> ☐ I can understand that we grow because our skeleton grows.
> ☐ I can measure the length of bones.
> ☐ I can say why it is better to measure in standard units.
> ☐ I can record data in a table.

1.3 Skeletons and movement

We are going to...

- explain how muscles work to make us move
- observe how muscles change when we move
- make a model to show how muscles work in pairs
- explain how the model is the same as and different to real muscles
- find out that movement is good for our health.

Getting started

1. Name some of the ways in which our body can move.
2. How does our skeleton help our body to move?

contract   relax

9

1 Living Things

Muscles make us move

Bones are strong and hard. They cannot bend, but your body can move in many ways.

All animals with skeletons have muscles attached to the bones. Muscles are the parts of the body that allow us to sit, stand, walk, run, bend and stretch. They make it possible for us to smile, hold a pen, eat and talk.

Muscles are found under the skin. They cover the skeleton and give your body the shape that you have.

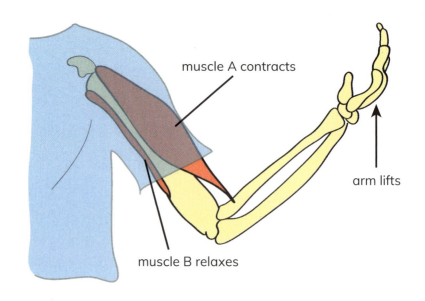

How muscles work

Muscles pull on bones to make them move. Muscles work by getting shorter and longer. When muscles get shorter they pull on the bones they are joined to. We say that the muscles **contract**. The pulling movement allows you to move and do the action that you want. When muscles **relax** they get longer and let you rest.

Muscles always work in pairs. One muscle contracts and pulls on the bone it is joined to. This makes the bone move. The other muscle relaxes.

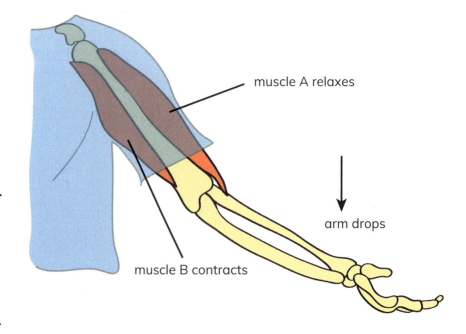

10

1.3 Skeletons and movement

> Activity
>
> **Find out how muscles work in pairs**
>
> > **You will need:**
> > something heavy to lift, such as a large book.
>
> - Look closely at the muscles in your arm. Also look at the pictures that show how the arm muscles work.
> - Hold the weight in one hand and slowly lift the weight up towards you.
> - Put your other hand over the front on your upper arm. Feel how the muscle changes as you lift the weight.
> - How does the muscle at the back of your arm feel?
> - Straighten your arm. Feel what happens to the muscle at the back of your arm.
> - What happens to the muscle at the front of your arm?
>
> **Questions**
>
> 1. When you pick up a heavy book, which muscle in your arm contracts? Which muscle in your arm relaxes? How do you know this from doing the activity?
> 2. How strong are your arm muscles? Think of a way to find out that will be a fair test.
> 3. How can we make our muscles bigger?
> 4. The heart is a special muscle that is not joined to any bones. Why do you think the heart is not joined to any bones?

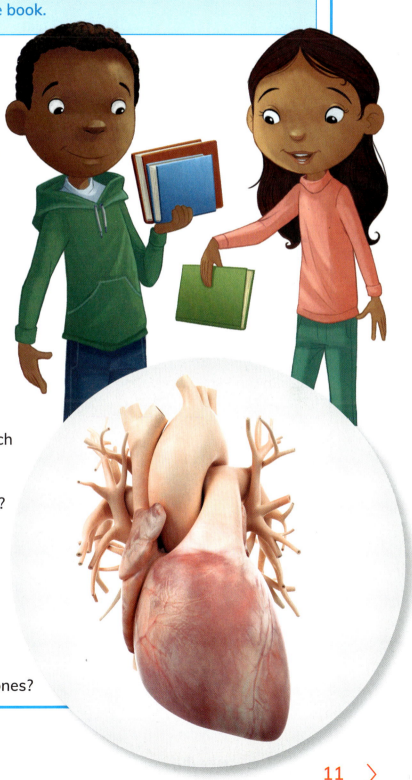

1 Living Things

Think like a scientist

Make a model of arm muscles

You will make a model to show how the muscles of the arms work in pairs.

> **You will need:**
> a piece of thick card, two elastic bands (one longer than the other), scissors, paper fastener (split pin), stapler and staples, a ruler, a piece of sticky tack or modelling clay.

- Cut two equal lengths of card about 20 cm long.
- For each piece of card, make a hole about 5 cm away from one end using the point of the scissors. Place a piece of sticky tack or Plasticine behind the card to push the scissors into.

card lengths

Be careful when making the hole with the scissors. You will need to push harder because the card is thick and your hand could slip and cut yourself. Take care with the sharp point of the split pin.

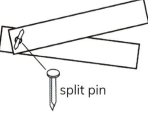
split pin

- Put the card pieces on top of each other with the holes lined up. Push the paper fastener through the holes to join the two pieces of card. This is your arm.
- Staple the longer elastic band to the inside of the upper and lower 'bones' of the card arm.
- Staple the shorter elastic band to the outside of the upper and lower 'bones' of the card arm. The elastic bands should be tight but not pulling.

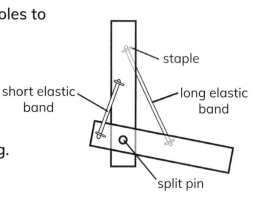

Questions

1. What happens to the card arm when you pull on the longer elastic band?
2. What happens to the card arm when you pull on the shorter elastic band?
3. Explain how the two elastic bands act like muscles in the body that lift and lower the arm.
4. a In what ways is your model the same as your arm muscles?
   b In what ways is your model different to your arm muscles?

Movement keeps us healthy

We use our muscles to move in different ways. We can walk, run, dance, lift things, climb and jump. Movement is good for our bodies. Sitting still for a long time is not good for our bodies.

Movement helps to keep us healthy in different ways.

Movement:

- makes your heart and lungs work better
- makes your muscles and bones stronger
- lets you stretch your body easily
- helps to stop you from getting some illnesses
- helps you think better
- puts you in a good mood.

Questions

1. Make a list of all the things you did today that made you move. Start from when you woke up.
2. a Which things did you do today that did not make you move, or made you move very little?
   b How much time every day do you spend sitting down and not moving?
3. Think of five different ways you can do more movement every day.

How can I use what I have learnt to be healthier?
Did I learn anything that I can share with other people?

13

1 Living Things

Look what I can do!

- ☐ I can understand that muscles work in pairs.
- ☐ I can explain how muscles work by pulling on bones.
- ☐ I can understand that when one muscle in a pair contracts, the other muscle in the pair relaxes.
- ☐ I can observe that muscles get shorter and fatter when they contract.
- ☐ I can observe that muscles get longer and thinner when they relax.
- ☐ I can use a model to show how muscles work.
- ☐ I can say how movement keeps us healthy.

> 1.4 Different kinds of skeletons

We are going to...

- learn about different kinds of skeletons
- find out the difference between vertebrates and invertebrates
- learn how to use an identification key
- use observations to group animals with and without an exoskeleton.

Getting started

1. Name some animals that have skeletons made of bone.
2. Your skeleton is inside your body. Do you think an animal can have a skeleton on the outside of its body?
3. Do you think the animal in the picture has a skeleton? Say why or why not.

exoskeleton
identification key
invertebrate
vertebrate

1 Living Things

Animals with bones

The animals in the pictures all have bones. They have a skeleton with a backbone inside their bodies. We call animals with skeleton inside their bodies **vertebrates**. The word vertebrate means 'with a backbone'.

We can sort vertebrates into five groups. See if you can identify the group that each of the animals in the pictures belongs to.

tiger

lizard

parrot

fish

frog

dolphin

16

- Fish are vertebrates that live in water. They have fins instead of arms and legs. Their bodies are covered with scales.
- Amphibians, such as frogs, live in water and on land. Their bodies are covered with a smooth, wet skin.
- Reptiles, such as snakes, lizards and tortoises, are covered with dry scales. Most reptiles live on land. Some reptiles live in water, for example crocodiles.
- Birds are covered with feathers. Birds have wings instead of arms. Most birds can fly. Some birds, like the ostrich, cannot fly.
- Mammals are covered with hair or fur. Most mammals live on land. Some mammals live in the sea, for example whales and dolphins.

Animals without bones

Some animals have no bones. Animals with no bones are called **invertebrates**. The word invertebrate means 'without a backbone'.

Some invertebrate animals have hard skins or shells on the outside of their bodies. This hard outer layer is called an **exoskeleton**. The exoskeleton protects the animal and supports the animal's body. Insects, such as locusts and beetles, have an exoskeleton.

Other invertebrate animals such as worms and jellyfish have soft bodies. These animals do not have an exoskeleton.

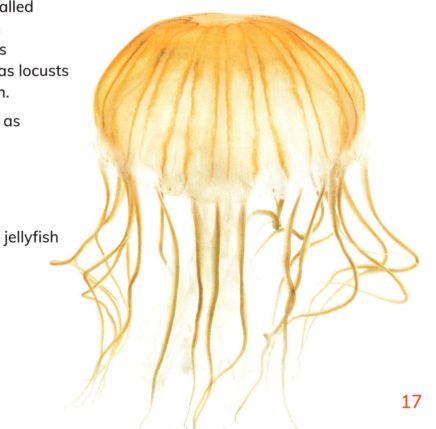

locust

jellyfish

1 Living Things

Questions

1. What is the difference between a vertebrate animal and an invertebrate animal?
2. Which of the animals in the pictures are vertebrates? Name another vertebrate you know of.
3. Which of the animals in the pictures are invertebrates? Name another invertebrate you know of.
4. Which of the invertebrates in the pictures have an exoskeleton?
5. The skeleton of a vertebrate grows, which allows the animal to grow. The exoskeleton of an invertebrate cannot grow. How do you think an invertebrate with an exoskeleton is able to grow?

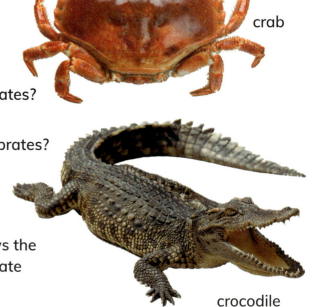

crab

crocodile

spider

beetle

goat

eagle

frog

earthworm

1.4 Different kinds of skeletons

Identification keys

Scientists use **identification keys** to help them sort and identify objects, materials and living things. Identification keys are based on questions that can be answered either 'yes' or 'no'. By answering the questions, we can identify and name animals, or sort them into the right groups.

Look at this example which identifies different types of vertebrates.

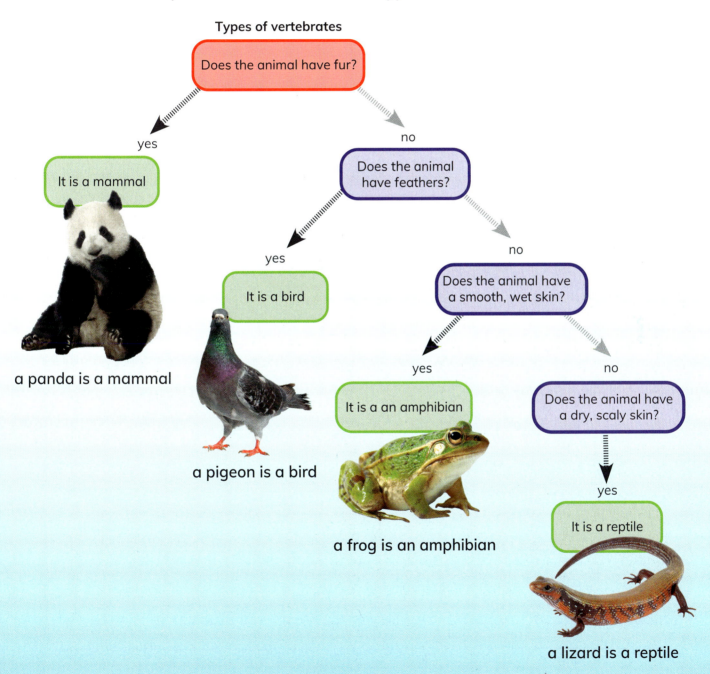

19

1 Living Things

Think like a scientist

Identify vertebrates and invertebrates

Look at the pictures of the animals. Some of the animals are vertebrates. Some of the animals are invertebrates.

Use the key to identify and name animals in the pictures.

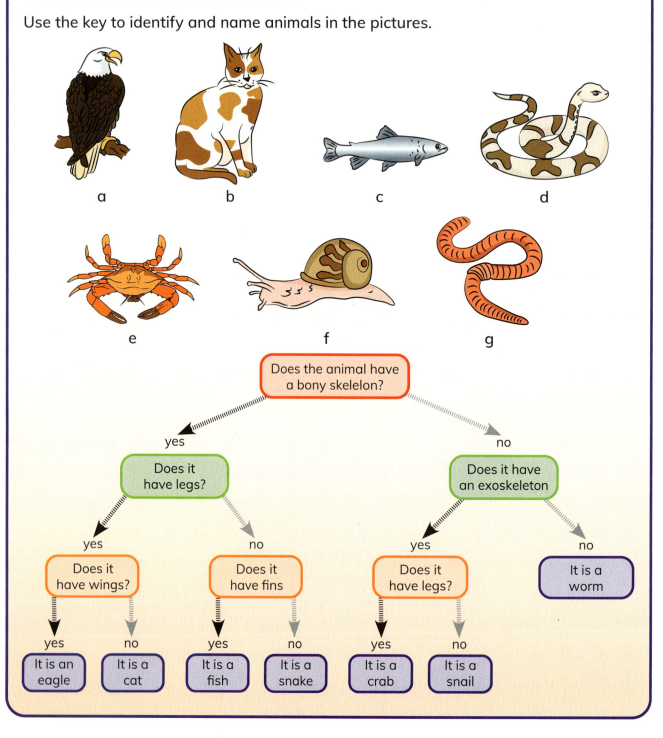

1.4 Different kinds of skeletons

> **Continued**
>
> **Questions**
>
> 1. Which animals in the key are vertebrates?
> 2. Which animals in the key are invertebrates?
> 3. a There are five groups of vertebrates. Can you name these five groups?
>   b Which group does each vertebrate you identified in the key belong to?
>
> **How am I doing?**
>
> How well can you use a key?
> Use different coloured cards to show how confident you feel using a key.
>
> 🟩 I get it! I can even explain to others.
>
> 🟨 I need a little more help.
>
> 🟥 I don't get it. I need a lot of help.

Look what I can do!

☐ I can identify vertebrates as animals with a backbone.
☐ I can identify invertebrates as animals without a backbone.
☐ I can identify invertebrates that have an exoskeleton.
☐ I can use an identification key.
☐ I can use observations to group animals with and without an exoskeleton.

1 Living Things

> 1.5 Medicines and infectious diseases

We are going to...
- learn why we take medicines
- describe how to take medicines safely
- find out that plants, animals and people can get infectious diseases
- learn that vaccinations can prevent some diseases in people and animals
- do research to answer questions about vaccinations.

Getting started

The girl in the picture is taking medicine.

1. Have you ever taken medicine? Why did you take it?
2. The girl is taking a liquid medicine. What other kinds of medicines do you know of?
3. Why do you think an adult is giving the medicine to the girl?

germs
infect
infectious disease
instructions
medicines
prevent
vaccinations

1.5 Medicines and infectious diseases

Medicines

We take **medicines** to help make us better when we have an illness. Some medicines stop us from getting ill. We say that these medicines **prevent** us from getting ill.

Taking medicines safely

Medicines make us better, but we have to take them safely and properly. You should only take medicines if they are given to you by a doctor, a nurse or an adult who looks after you. All medicines come with **instructions**. The instructions tell you how much medicine you must take and how often you should take it. We must always follow those instructions.

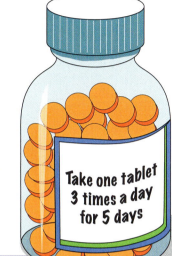

Take one tablet 3 times a day for 5 days

Think like a scientist 1

How to take medicines safely

Arun and his friends talked about how to take medicines safely. These are their ideas:

It's okay to take someone else's medicine if they have the same illness as you.

If you forget to take your medicine in the morning just take more at lunchtime.

If the instructions tell you to take the medicine with food, you must make sure that you do.

You must always take the right amount of medicine. If you take too much it can be harmful.

1 Living Things

> **Continued**
>
> 1. Discuss the things Arun and his friends are saying about how to take medicines safely.
> 2. Decide if Arun and his friends are right or not. You might need to do some research to find out more information about this.
> 3. Make an information sheet about how to take medicines safely. You can include any other information that you find about how to take medicines safely.

How we take medicines

We can take medicines in different ways.

We take some medicines as injections. Some injections can stop or prevent us from getting illnesses such as measles or flu. These injections are called **vaccinations**.

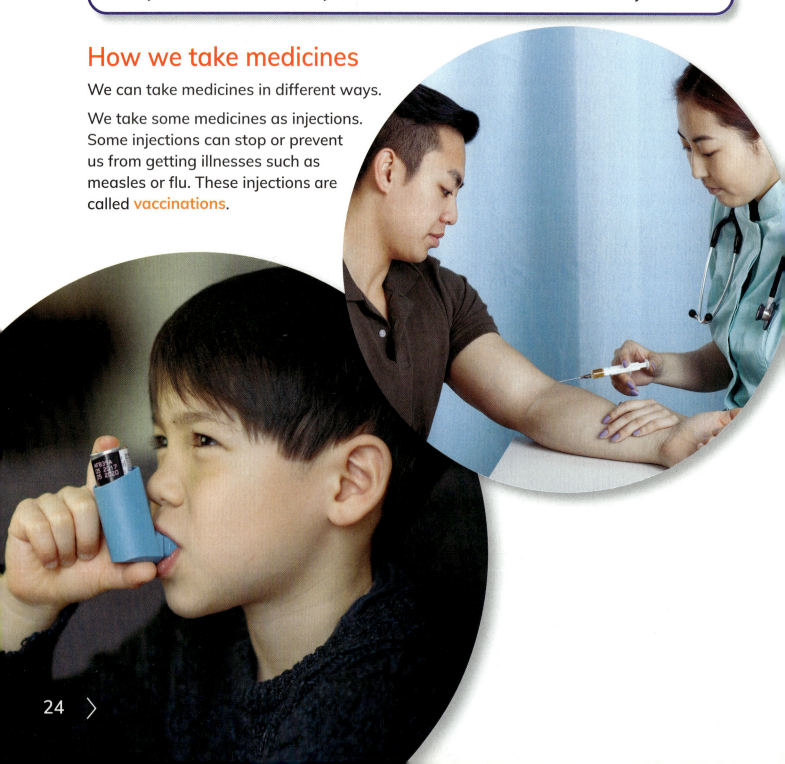

24

1.5 Medicines and infectious diseases

We breathe in medicines from inhalers for asthma and other breathing problems.

We use creams and ointments to stop insect bites itching and for skin problems.

People who are very sick in hospital often get their medicine directly into their blood through a drip.

Questions

1. Why do we take medicines?
2. Predict what you think would happen if you did not take all of the medicine the doctor gave you.
3. Do you think we can use a cream as a medicine for a sore throat?
   Say why or why not.
4. Why do you think people in hospital often get their medicine through a drip?

Think like a scientist 2

Research information about vaccinations

Vaccinations can prevent some infectious diseases in people.
Do some research to find out the following information about vaccinations.

History of vaccinations

- Who invented the first vaccinations?
- Which disease did the first vaccinations prevent?
- How were the vaccinations made and given?

1 Living Things

> **Continued**
>
> Vaccinations today
>
> - Is there a vaccination programme for children in your local area?
> - If so, which diseases are children vaccinated against?
> - How are the vaccinations for the different diseases given? For example, an injection to prevent 'flu.
> - How have the ways of giving vaccinations changed since the time of the first vaccination?
>
> Be prepared to share your findings with your class.

Infectious diseases

An **infectious disease** is a disease that is caused by very tiny living things we call **germs**. The germs **infect** your body. This means the germs get into your body and make you ill. We take medicines to kill the germs that infect our bodies.

People, animals and plants can all have infectious diseases. Flu, measles and malaria are some infectious diseases that humans can have.

Infectious diseases in plants can harm different parts of the plant. For example, leaf blast can kill young rice plants.

Bird flu is an infectious disease that infects birds, humans and other animals. Almost all birds that get bird flu die. Bird flu spreads easily from sick birds to healthy birds. The farmer in the picture is checking the chicken for signs of bird flu. Many farmers give vaccinations to their chickens, geese and ducks to prevent them from getting bird flu.

leaf blast disease

26

1.5 Medicines and infectious diseases

Questions

1. Say in your own words what an infectious disease is.
2. Why do you think the farmer in the picture wears gloves when she checks the chicken for signs of bird flu?
3. How can the farmer prevent the chicken from getting bird flu?

How can I use what I have learnt in the future?
Did I learn anything that can help other people?

Look what I can do!

- ☐ I can say why we take medicines.
- ☐ I can describe how to take medicines safely.
- ☐ I can understand that plants, animals and people can get infectious diseases.
- ☐ I can understand that vaccinations can prevent some diseases in people and animals.
- ☐ I can do research to answer questions about vaccinations.

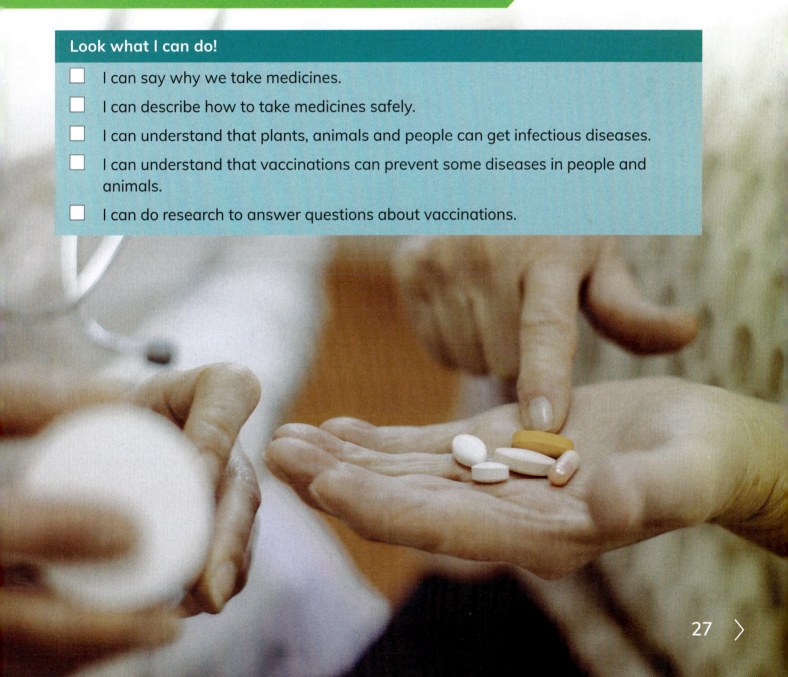

1 Living Things

Project: Earthworm farming

Earthworms are invertebrates. Earthworms live in the earth or soil.

People all over the world keep earthworm farms. They grow the earthworms in containers that are dark and moist inside, like the soil.

The farmers feed the worms with materials such as vegetable peels and garden waste. Earthworms leave droppings called 'castings'. The earthworms' castings form a substance called worm compost. The worm compost contain substances that help plants to grow better. The worm farmers sell the worm compost to gardeners and other farmers.

Activity

Work in pairs.

Speak to someone in your local area who farms earthworms.

These are some questions you could ask:

- Why did you decide to farm earthworms?
- Where do the earthworms live?
- What materials do the worms live in?
- Which foods do the earthworms like to eat?
- Which foods don't the earthworms like to eat?
- How much time does it take for the worm compost to form?
- How does the earthworm farm affect the environment?

You can also think of your own questions that you would like to ask.

Take photographs and make a PowerPoint presentation of your findings to show to the class.

What role did I have in this project?
Am I happy with the work I did?
What could I do differently next time to work better?

28

Check your progress

1. Write the word that describes each of the following:
    a. A frame made of bone that supports our body.
    b. The bones of the head.
    c. Something that shows us how another thing looks or works.
    d. The parts inside our bodies.
    e. Animals with no backbone.
    f. The parts of the body that allow our bones to move.
    g. The hard skin or shell on the outside of the body of some animals.
    h. An injection that prevents disease.

2. Look at the drawing and answer the questions.

    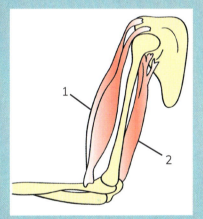

    a. Write down the number of the muscle that gets shorter to bend the arm.
    b. Choose the correct words in the sentences to explain how the muscle makes the arm bend upwards.

    The muscle **contracts / relaxes**. The muscle gets **longer / shorter** and **pushes / pulls** on the arm bone.

    c. What happens to the other muscle when the arm bends?

3. Look at the picture of a rabbit skeleton.

    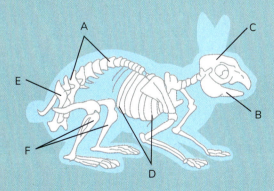

    a. Label parts A, B and C.
    b. Which part protects the animal's brain?
    c. What is the function of part D?
    d. Which part allows the animal to walk and hop?
    e. Which part is the hip bone?
    f. The skeleton protects body parts and helps the animal to move. Describe one other function of the skeleton.

1 Living Things

Continued

4   Arun recorded all the things he did for a day. He drew a graph to show the results.

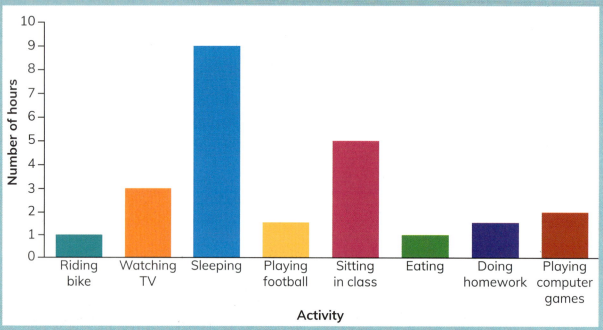

a   Which activity did Arun spend most time doing?

b   Which activities did Arun do for the shortest amount of time?

c   For how many hours did Arun do activities that made him move a lot?

d   Which activities could Arun do less of? Why?

e   Suggest two other activities that will make him do more movement.

f   Name three reasons why it is good for the body to be active and move.

5   Decide whether each of the statements is true.

a   Germs cause infectious diseases.

b   If you take more medicine you will get better faster.

c   Always follow the instructions on the medicine label.

d   It is OK to take medicine that a friend gives you.

e   Plants do have not any infectious diseases.

2 Energy

> 2.1 Energy around us

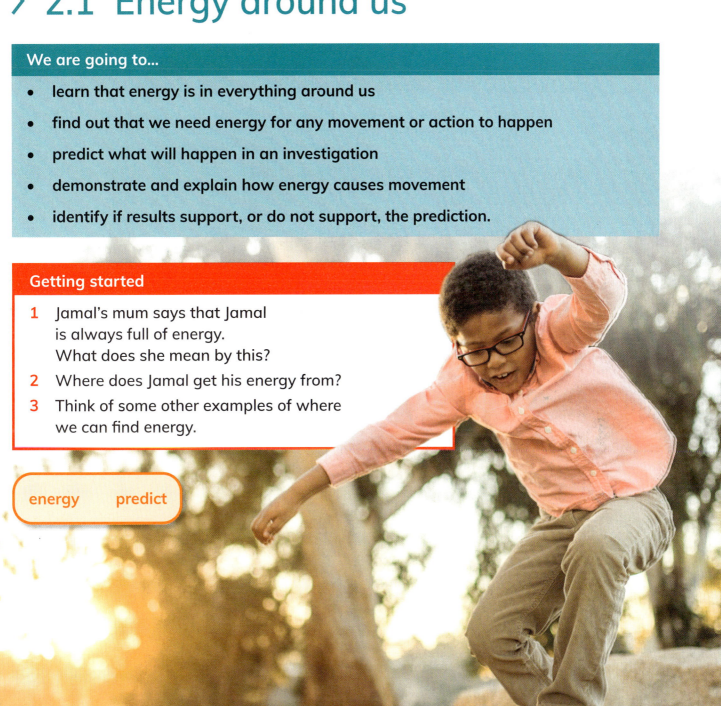

We are going to...

- learn that energy is in everything around us
- find out that we need energy for any movement or action to happen
- predict what will happen in an investigation
- demonstrate and explain how energy causes movement
- identify if results support, or do not support, the prediction.

Getting started

1. Jamal's mum says that Jamal is always full of energy. What does she mean by this?
2. Where does Jamal get his energy from?
3. Think of some other examples of where we can find energy.

energy   predict

2 Energy

Energy is all around us

Energy is everywhere around us.

Living things have energy. We get our energy from the food we eat. We use this energy to move, grow, breathe and carry out all our other life processes.

Non-living things also have energy. For example, there is energy in moving air that makes a wind turbine turn. There is also energy in light, heat and sound.

Light, heat and sound are forms of energy. Movement is also a form of energy.

Questions

1. Look at the pictures. Where is the energy in each picture?
2. What type of energy does each picture show?

 1
 2
 3
 4
 5

What is energy?

We know that everything has energy. We can't always see energy, but we can observe the things that energy does.

Energy makes things move. All moving things have energy.

Energy also makes things change. For example, a moving ball can break a window.

We can think of energy as anything that can cause movement or carry out an action. We need energy for everything we do.

2.1 Energy around us

Think like a scientist

Demonstrate what energy does

You will need: a ping pong ball or piece of paper crumpled into a ball

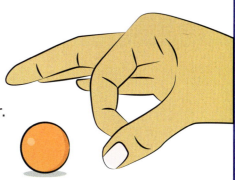

- Flick the ping pong ball with your finger. What happens?
- Why do you think this happens? Use the word energy in your answer.
- **Predict** what will happen if you flick the ball harder. Remember, a prediction is what we think will happen based on our knowledge and experience. Flick the ball.
- Was your prediction correct?
- Say why you think this happened.

Questions

1 Which objects in the activity had energy? Say how you know this.
2 a In the activity, which things did energy change?
  b How did the things change when you added more energy?
3 Suggest a way in the activity that you could show that moving air has energy.

How am I doing?

How well can I:	Very well 😊	Quite well 😐	I need help ☹
name three examples of energy around us?			
describe how I use energy to make a ball move?			

33

2 Energy

Look what I can do!

- ☐ I can understand that energy is in everything around us.
- ☐ I can understand that we need energy for any movement or action to happen.
- ☐ I can demonstrate and explain how energy causes movement.
- ☐ I can make a prediction in an investigation.
- ☐ I can identify if results support, or do not support, the prediction.

2.2 Energy transfers

We are going to...

- find out that energy can be transferred from one object to another object
- learn that energy does not get used up or disappear
- observe and describe energy transfers
- identify factors in a fair test
- think about why it is important to do fair test investigations
- think about how to work safely in an investigation
- think about how we can know if results are true
- identify energy transfers.

Getting started

1. What type of energy does a moving ball have?
2. Where does the energy come from to make the ball move?
3. Do objects that are not moving have energy? Give an example.

conclusion

energy transfer

35

2 Energy

Energy can move

Why does a cup get hot when you put hot water into it?

Heat energy makes things get hot. The hot water has heat energy. The heat energy in the hot water moves to the cup. This is an **energy transfer**. After a while, the cup and the water get colder. The heat energy does not get used up or disappear. The cup and the water get colder because the heat energy is transferred to other objects or into the surrounding environment.

We can think of the way energy moves from one object to as an energy chain. Here is an example of an energy chain for the transfer of heat energy from the water to the cup and surrounding environment.

water → cup → surrounding environment

Think like a scientist 1

Observe an energy transfer

You will need: a beaker of hot water, a metal teaspoon, a bead, petroleum jelly

- Put a small bit of petroleum jelly on the handle of the teaspoon. Push the bead into the petroleum jelly on the spoon.
- Your teacher will pour hot water into a beaker. Put the spoon in the beaker.

Be careful when near hot water. You don't want it to spill onto you.

- Observe what happens to the bead. Why does this happpen?
- Draw an energy chain for the energy transfers that took place.
- Suggest a question that you have investigated in this activity.
- Use your question to write a **conclusion** to say what you found out about energy transfers from the experiment. Remember that a conclusion is what you have found out in an investigation.

36

2.2 Energy transfers

Energy can be transferred from any object that contains energy. Think about the Sun. It gives off heat energy and light energy. That energy is transferred through space to the Earth so we have heat and light.

Think like a scientist 2

Plan a fair test on energy transfers

Zara made an observation.

- Ask a question to investigate Zara's observation.
- Suggest how you could do a fair test investigation to answer your question. Remember to think about which things you will change and which things you will keep the same. What will you measure?
- Why do we need to do fair tests in investigations?
- Identify any dangers in doing the investigation.
- How can you work safely in your investigation?
- How can you make sure that you do not make any mistakes when measuring?
- Suggest a way to present your results.

When I stir my tea with a metal teaspoon, the teaspoon gets hot. If I use a plastic teaspoon, the spoon does not get hot.

2 Energy

Activity

Identify energy transfers

Copy and fill in the table to identify the energy transfer in each of the pictures.

A  B  C  D

Type of energy transferred	Where the energy comes from	Where the energy is transferred to
A		
B		
C		
D		

How do you feel about today's lesson?

How did the practical work help you to learn today?

Look what I can do!

☐ I can understand that energy is transferred from one object to another object.
☐ I can understand that energy does not get used up or disappear.
☐ I can observe and describe energy transfers.
☐ I can identify factors in a fair test.
☐ I can say why it is important to do fair test investigations.
☐ I can suggest how to work safely in an investigation.
☐ I can suggest how we can know if results are true.
☐ I can identify energy transfers.

> 2.3 Energy changes

We are going to...

- observe that energy can change from one form to a different form
- find out that some energy is transferred from an object into the surrounding environment
- describe energy changes
- learn that we cannot make energy or destroy energy.

Getting started

1. How would you feel if you rode a bicycle fast for half an hour? Why would you feel like this?
2. Describe the energy transfer that makes the bicycle move.
3. Think about your answer to question 1. Name another form of energy that riding a bicycle produces.

destroy

electrical appliances

electrical energy

2 Energy

Energy can change form

We have seen that energy moves. Sometimes the energy changes form when it moves.

Think about hitting a drum. We use movement energy to hit the drum.
The energy moves from our hand to the drum.
The drum skin moves and the drum makes a sound.
This happens because the movement energy changes to sound energy.

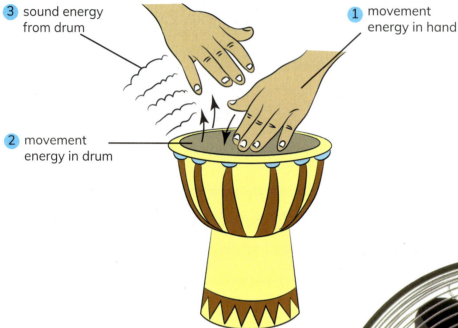

1 movement energy in hand
2 movement energy in drum
3 sound energy from drum

Electricity is another form of energy.
We call it **electrical energy**. There are often energy changes when we use **electrical appliances** such as stoves and fans. These are objects that need electrical energy to work. For example, a fan changes electrical energy into movement energy.

Not all the energy in an object moves to another object. In the fan, some of the movement energy changes into sound energy. The sound moves into the surrounding environment.

40

2.3 Energy changes

Think like a scientist

Observe energy changes

> **You will need:**
> a desk lamp, a paper spiral, thin string, a pencil

- Use the pencil to make hole in one end of the paper spiral.
- Thread the string through the hole.
- Tie a knot in the end of the string to hold the spiral in place. Tie the free end of string around the pencil.
- Turn the lamp over so that it shines upwards, towards the ceiling. Hold the spiral about 10 cm above the lamp.

Don't let the paper touch the lamp.

- Suggest another way you can work safely in this investigation.
- Observe and describe what happens.

Questions

1. A lamp gives off light. What other form of energy does the lamp give off?
2. What form of energy did you observe in the spiral when you held it over the lamp?
3. a Describe the energy transfer that happened in the experiment.
   b Describe the energy change that happened in the experiment.
4. Think of two energy changes that happen in electrical appliances. Say what form of energy from the appliance moves into the surrounding environment.

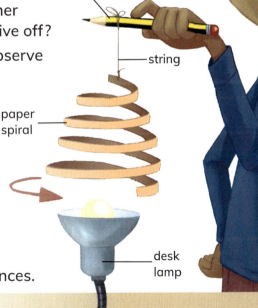

41

2 Energy

Where does the energy go?

Sometimes we can't observe any signs that an object has energy. It seems that energy is used up. This is not so. Energy cannot get used up. We also cannot **destroy** energy so that it disappears or no longer exists.

Energy can only be transferred and change form. For example, if we leave a cup of hot tea for a while, it gets cold. The heat energy in the tea is not used up or destroyed. Instead, the heat energy moves from the tea and cup to the surrounding environment.

In the same way, we cannot make energy. All the energy around us has always been with us and always will be with us. It just moves and changes form.

Questions

1. Why does it sometimes seem that energy is used up? Give an example.
2. If the energy is not used up or destroyed, where does it go?

What did you learn about energy changes?

What did you find difficult?

What would you like to know more about?

Look what I can do!

☐ I can understand that energy can change from one form of energy to a different form of energy.

☐ I can understand that energy moves from an object into the surrounding environment.

☐ I can describe energy changes.

☐ I can understand that we cannot make energy or destroy energy.

> 2.4 Energy and living things

We are going to...
- learn why living things need energy
- find out where living things get their energy from
- describe food chains
- make drawings of food chains to show energy transfers between living things.

Getting started
1. Why do our bodies need energy?
2. Do all living things need energy?
3. Where do living things get their energy from?

carnivore   omnivore
consumer   predator
food chain   prey
herbivore   producer

Living things need energy

All living things need energy. They need energy to move, to grow, to reproduce and to carry out other life processes. Plants and animals will not be healthy if they don't have enough energy.

We get our energy from the food we eat. The energy moves from the food into our bodies. We use that energy to live and be healthy.

Plants do not eat food to get their energy. Plants use light energy from the Sun to make or produce their food. We call plants **producers**. Plants are the only living things that can make their own food.

43

2 Energy

Animals need plants for energy

Animals including humans cannot make their food. They must eat, or consume, plants or other animals to get their food and energy. Animals including humans are called **consumers**.

Some animals eat plants only. We call animals that eat only plants **herbivores**. Zebras and snails are examples of herbivores.

Some animals eat other animals that eat plants. We call these animals **carnivores**. Carnivores eat herbivores. They also sometimes eat other carnivores. Tigers and owls are examples of carnivores.

Sometimes carnivores are called **predators**. The animals that carnivores kill and eat are called **prey**. For example, an owl that kills and eats a mouse is a predator. The mouse is the prey.

Animals that eat both plants and animals are called **omnivores**. For example, monkeys mostly eat plant leaves, fruits and seeds, but they also eat insects and other small animals.

Questions

1. Why are plants called producers?
2. Why are animals called consumers?
3. a What is the difference between predators and prey? Give an example in your answer.
   b In what way are predators and prey similar?
   c Can a herbivore be a predator? Say why or why not.

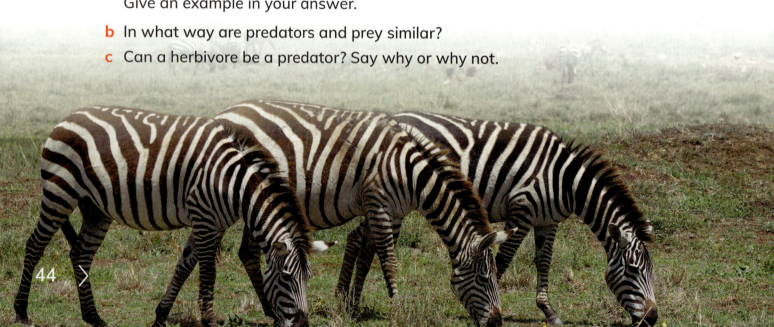

2.4 Energy and living things

Food chains

A **food chain** shows the order in which animals eat plants and other animals to get energy. Food chains always contain a producer and at least one consumer. Energy is always transferred from the producer to the consumer because the consumer eats the producer. Look at the examples.

In food chain 1, the corn is the producer and the hen is the consumer.

Identify the producer and the consumer in food chain 2.

We can show a food chain as a drawing. When we draw a food chain, we show the order in which food, and the energy it contains, are transferred from one living thing to the next. The order of living things in a food chain is always:

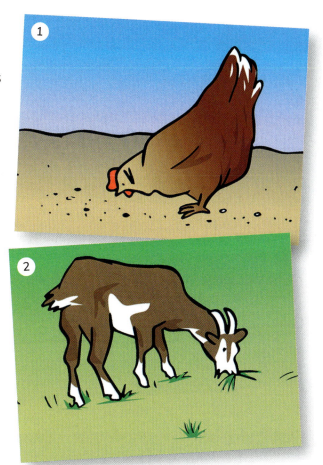

producer → consumer

The arrows in the food chain show the direction in which the energy in the food is transferred.

This is the drawing of food chain 1:

corn → hen

If a boy eats the hen in food chain 1, he is another consumer. So now the food chain is:

corn → hen → boy

Questions

Here is a list of living things: tiger, palm tree, snail, crocodile, rice plant, cow, person.

1 Which of the living things are:

   a producers?   b consumers?

2 Which living things in the list are:

   a herbivores?   b carnivores?

3 Which consumer do you think is an omnivore? Say why.

45

2 Energy

Think like a scientist

Draw food chains

1 Put the living things in the right order to make food chains.
   Draw the food chains.

   a   tomato, cat, bird

   b   frog, grasshopper, snake, rice plant

2 Draw a food chain of your own that includes a person as the
   second consumer.

3 Describe the energy transfers in your food chain.

How will you learn the different types of consumers?

Can you think of a way to help you remember them?

Look what I can do!

- [ ] I can say why living things need energy.
- [ ] I can say where living things get their energy from.
- [ ] I can describe food chains.
- [ ] I can make drawings of food chains to show energy transfers between living things.
- [ ] I can classify consumers as herbivores, omnivores, carnivores, predators and/or prey.
- [ ] I can explain how food chains show the order in which animals eat plants or other animals.

2.4 Energy and living things

Project: Find out how electricity is made

Most of the electricity that we use in our homes comes from power stations. A power station needs a source of energy to make electricity. In many countries, the energy used in power stations comes from burning coal. Coal is a fuel that stores energy. Other sources of energy for power stations can be fast-moving water, sunlight, nuclear material or natural gas.

Activity

1. Work in pairs. Speak to people, or do some research, to find out the following information about how electricity is made in your area:
   - What source of energy is used to make the electricity?
   - How does the form of energy change to make the electricity?
   - What are the different steps in making the electricity?
   - How does the electricity get into our homes?

   Make a poster or information sheet with drawings or photos to present your findings.

2. As a class, discuss how making electricity affects your local environment. How does it help the environment or harm the environment?

47

2 Energy

Check your progress

1. Write a list of the words in Column A. Choose the correct meaning for each word from column B. Write the correct meanings beside each word.

A	B
Energy	a living thing that gets its energy from eating other living things
Transfer	a living thing that gets its energy from the food it makes itself
Food chain	anything that can cause movement or carry out an action
Producer	a drawing that shows how energy moves from one living thing to another
Consumer	when something moves from one thing or place to another

2. Identify the energy changes in each of the pictures.

3. a Write these food chains so that the living things are in the correct order.

   bird → caterpillar → leaf

   eagle → grass → rabbit

   beetle → lizard → seeds → snake

   b What do the arrows in the food chains show?

4. Name three predators and their prey from the living things in question 3.

48

3 Materials

> 3.1 Materials, substances and particles

We are going to...

- find out the difference between materials, substances and particles
- show that particles move all the time
- learn that the particle model of matter describes the differences between substances that are solids, liquids and gases
- describe the particle model for solids and liquids
- play a game to demonstrate how solids and liquids are different.

Getting started

Look around the classroom and find different materials.

1. Which materials are solids?
2. Are there materials that are liquids or gases? If there are, name them.
3. How did you decide if each material was a solid, a liquid or a gas?

compare   particle
material   substance

49

3 Materials

Materials, substances and particles

Objects can be made of different types of materials.
For example, a school desk can be made of wood and metal.

Plastic, wood, rubber and glass are also materials. All materials are made of matter. Matter is everything around us. A material is a certain type of matter.

Most materials are mixtures of different substances.
A substance is a pure type of solid, liquid or gas. It is not a mixture.
For example:

- Salt is a solid substance.
- Pure water is a liquid substance.
- Oxygen is a substance that is a gas.

Glass is a material. To make glass, people mix sand with substances, such as soda ash and limestone. When they are heated together, they form a clear liquid glass.

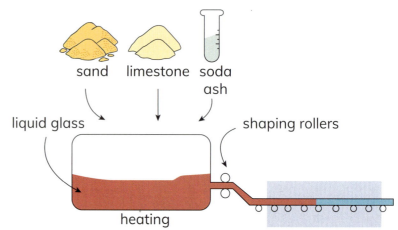

The liquid glass can be made into different shapes.
The liquid glass goes hard when it cools. People can use glass to make window panes, bottles and light bulbs.

3.1 Materials, substances and particles

All matter is made up of particles. A particle is a very small part or bit of something. Some particles are big enough for us to see, such as particles of dust. Most particles are much too small for us to see.

Questions

4 What is matter?

5 Explain the difference between a material and a substance.

6 Is glass a material or a substance? Say why.

7 a How are sand and pure water similar?

   b How are they different?

The particle model of matter

Because most particles of matter are very small, scientists use a model to explain how the particles form substances. The particle model describes the differences between substances that are solids, liquids and gases.

Scientists have found out some important things about the particles that make up solids, liquids and gases:

- The particles have spaces between them. When the spaces between the particles are small, the particles are held close together.

- The particles are always moving, even though we can't see them move. The amount of movement of the particles decides whether the substance is a solid, liquid or gas.

Think like a scientist

Demonstrate that particles of liquids move

You will need:
a beaker or glass jar, water, liquid food dye or colouring, a measuring cylinder or measuring cup

- Measure 100 ml of cold water into a beaker.
- Shake a few drops of food colouring into the beaker of water. Do not stir the water or move the beaker. Observe what happens.

51

3 Materials

> **Continued**
> - Make a drawing to record what happens in each beaker.
> - Label your drawing with these labels: beaker/jar, water, food dye.
> - Write a sentence to explain what you observed.
> - Say which type of scientific enquiry you used in the activity.

The drawings show scientists' ideas about the particle model for solids and liquids.

In solids, the particles are packed tightly together in a regular pattern, with the same amount of space between each particle. The spaces between the particles are very small. This means the particles cannot move around very much and are in a fixed position.

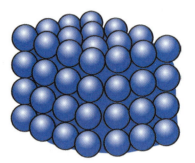

In a solid, the particles are packed tightly together

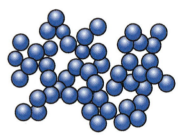

In a liquid, the particles are not packed in a regular pattern

In liquids, the particles are also close together, but they are not packed in a regular pattern. There are bigger spaces between the particles. This allows the particles to slide past one another and change places.

Activity

Play the particle game

In your class, divide into groups of four or five. Imagine that each person is a particle in a solid or a liquid.

Look at the pictures to see what to do.

solid

liquid

52

3.1 Materials, substances and particles

Continued

- Try to shake from side to side. What do you notice?
- Try to move closer together or further apart. What do you notice?
- Try to change the shape of your group. What do you notice?
- Now change group and do the activity again.

Questions

1 **Compare** what happened when you tried to shake as 'solids' and 'liquids'.

2 Compare what happened when you tried to move closer together or further apart as 'solids' and 'liquids'.

3 Compare what happened when you tried to change the shape of your group as 'solids' and 'liquids'.

4 How does the particle game demonstrate the particle model of matter?

How am I doing?

Answer 'Very well', 'Quite well' or 'I need help' to these questions:

- How well can I say how materials, substances and particles are different?
- How well can I describe the particle model of matter for solids and liquids?
- How well can I use a game to show the difference between solids and liquids?

Look what I can do!

☐ I can understand the difference between materials, substances and particles.

☐ I can understand that particles move all the time.

☐ I can understand that the particle model of matter describes the differences between solids, liquids and gases.

☐ I can describe the particle model for solids and liquids.

☐ I can demonstrate in a game how solids and liquids are different.

3 Materials

> 3.2 How do solids and liquids behave?

We are going to...

- use the particle model to explain how solids and liquids behave
- ask a question to investigate, choose which equipment to use in an investigation, measure time, collect and record measurements in a table, draw a bar graph of results and describe a pattern in results
- draw pictures of observations and write a conclusion about observations
- describe and explain how some solids can behave like liquids
- think about how we can use patterns in results in other investigations
- say how we can make sure our measurements are reliable
- think about why we use standard units of measurement.

pour   property   powder

Getting started

Say if each of these statements is true or false:

- All substances are made from particles.
- Materials are not made from particles.
- Particles in solids cannot move.
- Particles in liquids can slide past one another.
- There are always space between particles.

Properties of solids and liquids

A property describes what a substance or material is like, or how it behaves. We can measure, see or feel the properties of a substance or material. Solids and liquids have different properties.

54

3.2 How do solids and liquids behave?

Solids

Try to squeeze your desk, chair or pencil. Can you make it a different shape?

Solids keep their shape unless a force is exerted on them. The shape of a solid does not change on its own. We can make some solids change shape if we squeeze or push on them hard enough. Remember the particle model. Particles in a solid are packed closely together. There is no space for the particles to take on a different shape.

Liquids

Solids keep their shape. What about liquids?
What shape is a liquid inside a drinking glass?

Predict what will happen when you **pour** some water on to a flat surface.

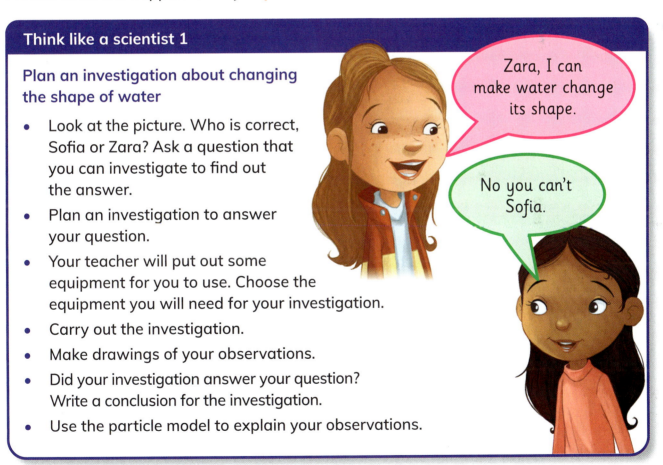

Think like a scientist 1

Plan an investigation about changing the shape of water

- Look at the picture. Who is correct, Sofia or Zara? Ask a question that you can investigate to find out the answer.
- Plan an investigation to answer your question.
- Your teacher will put out some equipment for you to use. Choose the equipment you will need for your investigation.
- Carry out the investigation.
- Make drawings of your observations.
- Did your investigation answer your question? Write a conclusion for the investigation.
- Use the particle model to explain your observations.

Liquid particles are further apart than solid particles. This lets them move around more easily. Since the particles can move, the liquid can flow and take the shape of its container.

3 Materials

Can solids behave like liquids?

We can pour a liquid. Can we pour a solid?

Most solids are hard and cannot change their shape because their particles are packed tightly together. This means that we cannot pour solids like we can pour liquids.

Some solids, such as sand, flour, salt and sugar, are similar to liquids. We can pour them and they take the shape of the container they are in. These solids are sometimes called powders.

Powders are made up of lots of very tiny pieces or grains. There is air between the grains, which means that the grains have space to move into. This lets the grains flow past one another like the particles in a liquid. But each grain of the powder is still made up of millions of particles that are too small for us to see.

Think like a scientist 2

Investigate solids that can flow

> **You will need:** a filter funnel, a measuring cup or measuring cylinder, a beaker or jar, salt, sugar, flour and sand, timer, a magnifying glass, paper

- Place a small amount of each solid onto a piece of paper. Feel each solid. Does it feel rough or smooth?
- Observe each solid with a magnifying glass. Does the solid have big grains or small grains?
- Measure 100 ml of a solid.
- Hold the funnel over the beaker or jar. Pour the solid into the funnel.
- Time how long it takes for the solid to flow through the funnel into the beaker.
- Repeat the steps with the other solids.
- Draw a graph to present your results.

3.2 How do solids and liquids behave?

Continued

Questions

1 Which solid flowed fastest?
2 Which solid flowed slowest?
3 Describe any difference you observe in the solids that flowed fastest and slowest.
4 Describe any the pattern you can see in your results.
5 How could you use the pattern you observed to predict how fast a different powder solid will flow?
6 Results are reliable if we get the same or similar answer each time we repeat a test or investigation. Do you think your results are reliable? How can you find out?
7 Which units did you use to measure time? How would this help you to compare your results with other groups' results?

How am I doing?

How well can you use the particle model to explain the properties of solids and liquids?

- I get it! I can even explain to others.
- I need a little more help.
- I don't get it. I need a lot of help.

Look what I can do!

- ☐ I can use the particle model to explain how solids and liquids behave.
- ☐ I can ask a question to investigate, choose which equipment to use in an investigation, measure time, collect and record measurements in a table, draw a bar graph of results and describe a pattern in results.
- ☐ I can draw pictures of my observations and write a conclusion about my observations.
- ☐ I can describe how some solids can behave like liquids.
- ☐ I can say how we can use patterns in results in other investigations.
- ☐ I can say how we can make sure our measurements are reliable.
- ☐ I can say why we use standard units of measurement.

3 Materials

> 3.3 Melting and solidifying

We are going to...
- describe melting and solidifying
- use the particle model to describe change of state
- learn that change of state is a physical process that does not change the type of substance
- make a prediction for an investigation and identify factors in a fair test.

Getting started
1. What different properties do solids and liquids have?
2. Do you think a solid can become a liquid? Give an example.
3. Do you think a liquid can become a solid? Give an example.

change of state   physical process
melting   solidifying

Change of state

Most materials and substances can change from one form to another when they are heated or cooled. This is called **change of state**. Solids, liquids and gases are different states of matter.

Sabera's ice-cream started as a solid. When the Sun heated the ice-cream it changed to a liquid. This change of state from solid to liquid is called **melting**.

We can show melting in this way:

solid —— heating causes melting ——▸ liquid

3.3 Melting and solidifying

Solidifying is the opposite of melting. Solidifying is when a substance or material changes from a liquid to a solid. Liquid substances solidify when they lose heat.

We can show solidifying in this way:

liquid ⎯⎯⎯ cooling causes solidifying ⎯⎯⎯→ solid

Solidifying is sometimes called freezing. This is because some liquids, like water, must be very cold before they can change into solids.

Think like a scientist 1

What happens to ice when it is heated?

You will need: ice cubes, a saucer

- Put an ice cube on the saucer. Is the ice liquid or solid? How do you know?
- Touch the ice. Does it feel hot or cold?
- Hold the ice cube in your hand over the saucer.
- Predict what you think will happen to the ice.
- What does happen to the ice? Was your prediction correct?

The change of state that happens when you heat the ice is:

solid state (ice) ⎯⎯⎯ heat ⎯⎯⎯→ liquid state (water)

Questions

1. What made the ice change state?
2. Did the ice change into another substance? Give a reason for your answer.
3. a Say how you can change the liquid water back into ice.
   b What is the process called when a substance changes state from a liquid to a solid?

Substances change state when they melt or solidify. Change of state is called a **physical process** because the substance only changes its form. The substance does not change into a different substance.

59

3 Materials

Change of state and the particle model

We know that the particles in solids and liquids are always moving. The particles in solids cannot move very much because they are tightly packed together.

The particles in a substance gain energy when we heat the substance. Some of the heat energy changes to movement energy. This makes the particles move faster. With enough energy, particles move so fast that they move away from each other. When this happens in a solid, the solid melts and becomes a liquid.

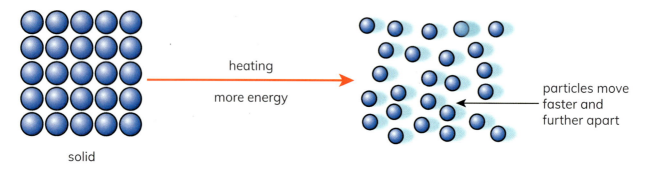

When a liquid loses heat energy and cools, its particles slow down and move closer together. If the particles lose enough energy, the liquid changes state and becomes a solid.

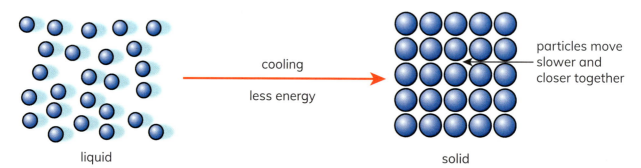

3.3 Melting and solidifying

Think like a scientist 2

Compare melting in different solids

You will need:
an ice cube, a square of chocolate, a cube of butter, three saucers, watch or timer

- Place an ice cube on a saucer. Do the same with the chocolate and the butter.
- Place the saucers in a warm place, such as on a sunny windowsill.
- Predict which solid will melt first.
- Observe the saucers every five minutes for 15 minutes.

Questions

1 Why did you place the solids in a warm place to make them melt?

2 Which solid melted first? Was your prediction correct?

3 Which solid took longest to melt?

4 Use the particle model to describe the change of state that each solid went through when you heated it.

5 Was this investigation a fair test? Say why or why not.

6 Write a conclusion for your investigation.

7 What will happen to the melted ice if you continue heating it?

61

3 Materials

Metals like gold and silver will also melt if they are heated enough. Metals must be heated to very high temperatures to make them melt. When the melted metal cools, it solidifies and forms a solid again.

What did you learn about change of state?

What did you find difficult?

What did you find easy?

Look what I can do!

☐ I can describe melting and solidifying.

☐ I can understand that change of state is a physical process that does not change the type of substance.

☐ I can use the particle model to describe change of state.

☐ I can make a prediction for an investigation and identify factors in a fair test.

> 3.4 Chemical reactions

> **We are going to...**
>
> - find out that new substances form in chemical reactions
> - make a prediction for an investigation
> - making drawings of observations
> - make a conclusion for an investigation
> - find out that we can obtain results by observing over time
> - research information to answer a scientific question.

Getting started

1. What happens to chocolate when you heat it?
2. Does the chocolate change in any other way? Give a reason for your answer.
3. Can you change the chocolate back to the way it was before you heated it? Say how.
4. a If you mix nuts with the heated chocolate, does the chocolate change into a new substance? Say why or why not.
   b Can you take the nuts out of the chocolate? How?

chemical reaction
react
rust

63

3 Materials

Making new substances

Change of state is a physical process that changes the form of a substance. The substance does not change. But when some substances are mixed together, they change and form a new substance or material. This is called a **chemical reaction**. We say that the substances **react** together.

Lots of chemical reactions take place around us every day. For example, when builders mix cement powder with sand, water and limestone, they make a new material called concrete. It is not possible to turn concrete back into the substances that made it. This is true for most chemical reactions.

Burning wood is also a chemical reaction. When we heat the wood, it reacts with the air. A grey substance called ash and two different gases form. The ash and gases are new substances.

Have you ever noticed that old tin cans and cars turn a reddish-brown colour if they are left outside for a long time? The metal in the cans and cars reacts with other substances to form a new substance called **rust**. Rusting is a chemical reaction.

3.4 Chemical reactions

Think like a scientist

Which substances react to form rust?

You will need:
three pieces of wire wool, three glass jars and one lid, water, a marking pen

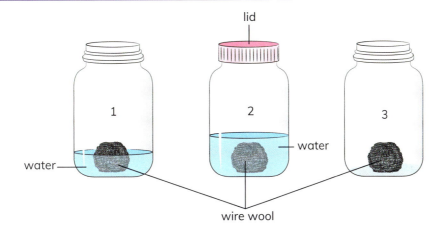

- Put a piece of wire wool in each jar. Number the jars 1, 2 and 3 with the marking pen.
- Pour enough water into jar 1 to cover some of the wire wool.
- Cover the wire wool in jar 2 with water. Put a lid on the jar.
- Leave jar 3 open.
- Predict what you think will happen in each jar.
- Observe the jars again after two days. Make drawings of your observations.

Questions

1 a In which jar or jars did the wire wool rust?
   b Was your prediction correct?
2 a Why did you need to wait two days to observe the jars?
   b What do you think will change if you wait another two days and then observe the jars again?
3 Make a conclusion for this investigation. Say why you made this conclusion.
4 Which type of scientific enquiry did you use in the investigation?

How did the practical work help you to learn about chemical reactions?

3 Materials

Activity

How can we prevent rusting?

Rusting is a problem almost everywhere in the world. Rust damages cars, buildings, bridges and many other things made of certain metals. The rust makes them weak.

- Do some research to find out about different ways in which people can stop rusting.
- Say how you think preventing rusting can help the environment in your local area.
- Present your findings to the class.

Look what I can do!

- ☐ I know that new substances form in chemical reactions.
- ☐ I can make a prediction for an investigation.
- ☐ I can make drawings of observations.
- ☐ I can make a conclusion for an investigation.
- ☐ I can understand that we can obtain results by observing over time.
- ☐ I can research information to answer a scientific question.

Project: Frozen foods

Have you ever eaten ice cream? Ice cream is a frozen food. We can buy many different foods that are frozen.

Part 1

Speak to people in your community who use frozen foods, or do some research in shops to find out:

- why people freeze foods
- which foods are often frozen
- how people prepare the frozen foods for eating.

Part 2

1. Plan an investigation to find out how much time it takes for different foods to freeze. Choose a question to investigate, such as:
   - Which liquids freeze quickest?
   - Do solid foods freeze faster than liquids?

   You can think of your own question to investigate, if you wish.

2. Choose the materials and equipment you will need. Here are some ideas.
   You should test five or six different foods.

3. Think about:
   - the factors you will keep the same and the factors you will change to make your investigation a fair test
   - how often you need to check if the foods are frozen, for example every 30 minutes or every hour
   - how you will test if the food is frozen or not
   - how you will record your results.

4. Carry out your investigation.
5. Draw a graph of your results.
6. Make a conclusion for your investigation based on your results and the question you investigated.

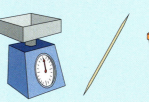

Part 3

Prepare a presentation to tell your class about your findings from Part 1 and Part 2 of this project. Your presentation should include pictures, graphs or drawings.

3 Materials

Check your progress

1 Say whether each of these statements describes a solid, a liquid, or both.
   a It is made of particles.
   b It cannot change shape easily.
   c It takes on the shape of its container.
   d It has very small spaces between particles.
   e Its particles are always moving.
   f It melts if it is heated.
   g Water is an example.

2 a Does the drawing represent a solid or a liquid?
   b Give two reasons for your answer.

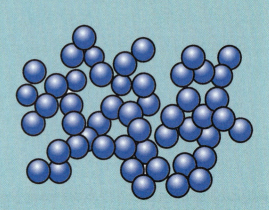

3 Mrs Pather poured some flour into a bowl to make some rotis.
   a Is flour a liquid or a solid?
   b Write two or three sentences to explain why she was able to pour the flour. Use these words:

grains   air   space   move   flow   liquid

4 Arun and Marcus want to compare how much time it takes to melt margarine and butter.
   a They want to plan a fair test. Which of these actions they should take? You can choose more than one.
      i Put equal amounts of butter and margarine together in a pan.
      ii Put equal amounts of butter and margarine in a pan and a pot.
      iii Put equal amounts of butter and margarine in two identical pans.
      iv Heat both pans one after the other on the same stove.
      v Heat each pan on an identical stove starting at the same time.
      vi Heat one pan on a gas ring and the other pan on an electric plate starting at the same time.
   b Draw diagrams to describe how the butter changes from a solid to a liquid. Use the particle model in your diagrams.

Check your progress

Continued

5 Sofia put a metal nail into a saucer of water. After three days she observed that the nail was covered in a reddish-brown substance.

   a   What is the reddish-brown substance?
   b   What three substances are needed for it to form?
   c   Why can the reddish-brown substance be a problem?
   d   What do we call the kind of process that forms new substances?

69

4 Earth and its habitats

> 4.1 The structure of the Earth

We are going to...

- describe a model of the structure of the Earth

- discuss how a model can never be a true copy of the real thing.

Getting started

This photograph of Earth was taken from space.

1 What shape is the Earth?

2 What does the surface of the Earth consist of?

3 What do you think might be underneath the surface?

4 The solid white part at the bottom of the image is ice. Use the particle model to describe how the ice becomes water in the blue parts of the image. What do we call this change?

5 What provides the energy that makes the ice change into water?

core

crust

external structure

internal structure

magma

mantle

70 >

4.1 The structure of the Earth

What is inside the Earth?

You already know that the outside part of the Earth is made of rocks and sea water. We call this the Earth's external structure.

But how can scientists find out about the parts of the Earth that are below the surface? These parts make up the Earth's internal structure. They can't cut the Earth in half and look at the structure inside. So they have to use a model to show the internal structure.

Remember we often use models in science. Sometimes models help us to understand how something works. Or models can help us to see what something looks like that we can't see in real life.

To look at the internal structure of the Earth, our model needs to show what the Earth would look like if we could cut it open, like we do with a peach. Here is a whole peach and a peach that has been cut open to see the inside.

Questions

1. Describe the external structure of a peach.
2. Does the right-hand image show the external structure or the internal structure of a peach?
3. Name the two layers which make up the internal structure of a peach.

71

4 Earth and its habitats

Here is a diagram to show the internal structure of the Earth.

The structure is made up of different layers: the crust, the mantle and the core.

Crust

The crust is the thin outer layer of the Earth where we live. The crust is formed of rocks. Under the oceans the crust is about 5 km thick. Under the land the crust is about 70 km thick. The temperature of the crust increases from 20 °C at the surface to 400 °C at its deepest part.

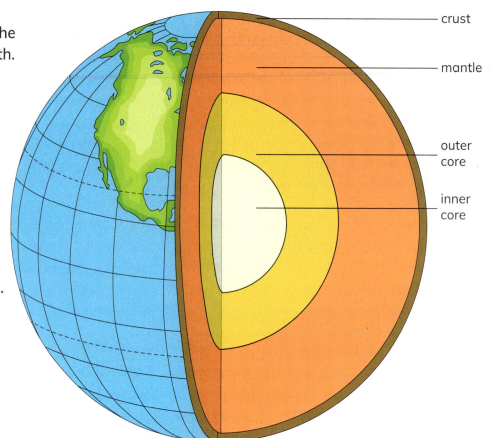

Mantle

The mantle is about 3000 km deep. Think of a distance that is 3000 km long. This is a much thicker layer than the crust. The rocks in the mantle have been melted by heat. The melted rocks are called magma. The magma can move like a liquid. The temperature rises to 1000 °C.

Core

The core is about 3400 km thick. The core is made up of the metals iron and nickel. The metals in the outer core are liquid.

The inner core is solid because of the pressure of all the other layers. For a long time scientists thought the temperature of the inner core was 5000 °C. In 2014, scientists used new equipment in a laboratory. They measured the temperature when iron melted under pressure. They found it was 6000 °C. This is as hot as the surface of the Sun!

4.1 The structure of the Earth

Activity

Summarise the structure of the Earth

Copy the table. Some information is filled in already. Use information from the diagram and information about the structure of the Earth to complete the table.

Name of layer	Crust		
Thickness		3000 km	
Material			Iron and nickel
Temperature			5000 – 6000 °C
Solid or liquid?	Solid		

How am I doing?

Exchange your completed table with a partner. Check any differences with your teacher.

Think like a scientist

Use a model to explain the structure of the Earth

Sofia is trying to explain the structure of the Earth to her friend Zara. She uses a peach as a model of the Earth. Discuss the answers to these questions.

1 Do you think the whole peach is a good model of the whole Earth? How is it a good or a bad model?

2 Sofia cuts the peach in half. The cut surface shows the layers in the internal structure of the peach. As a model of the Earth, which parts of the peach represent the crust, the mantle and the inner core?

3 Discuss ways in which the diagram of the inside of the peach is a good model or a bad model of the Earth's internal structure.

4 Read about the internal structure of the Earth again. Find an example of how information we have about the structure of the Earth changes over time.

5 Why is it very hot working in a deep mine?

How am I doing?

Explain the internal structure of the Earth to a younger person, such as a brother or sister. Use a model such as a round fruit.

73

4 Earth and its habitats

Look what I can do!

- [ ] I can use a model to describe the internal structure of the Earth.
- [ ] I know that a model can never be a true copy of the real thing.
- [ ] I can name and describe the layers of the interior of the Earth.

4.2 Volcanoes

> 4.2 Volcanoes

We are going to...

- identify features of volcanoes from pictures and diagrams
- draw a diagram to represent a volcano
- describe where volcanoes erupt at breaks in the Earth's crust.

Getting started

1 What is the layer below the Earth's crust called?
2 What material does this layer consist of?
3 Describe this material.

ash	erupt	risk
composite volcano	lava	secondary cone
crater	plateau	vent

How do volcanoes happen?

Sometimes a big crack develops in the Earth's crust. Magma from the mantle travels up the crack and shoots out or erupts on the surface of the Earth. This is called a volcano. Once the magma erupts on to the surface, the magma is called lava.

Different types of volcano

Lava can be very hot, sometimes 1000°C. When it is very hot, the lava flows quickly over the surface of the Earth. Eventually the lava will stop flowing, and then it cools and hardens into rocks. The islands of Hawaii in the Pacific Ocean are made of layers of lava. The lava has flowed, cooled and hardened into rocks. The layers of lava form a flat surface called a volcanic plateau.

75 >

4 Earth and its habitats

Besides lava, some volcanoes send out rocks, volcanic ash and gases. All these materials flow up a central pipe, or **vent**. During the eruptions, the vent widens at the surface to form a **crater**.

The most common type of volcano is a **composite volcano**. It has layers of **ash** and lava. The ash is burnt lava. The ash and lava build up a cone-shaped mountain with smooth sides. Some of the magma forces its way through cracks in the sides of the volcano. When this magma erupts it forms baby volcanoes called **secondary cones**.

Questions

Look at the photograph of flowing lava.

1. Point to the lava that is still flowing.
2. Point to the lava that has cooled down and hardened into rocks.

Look at the diagram of a volcano and the photograph of a volcano. The diagram is a model of the real thing.

3. Talk about features of the volcano that you can see on the photograph and the diagram.

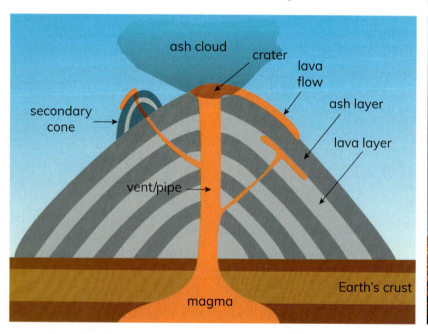

76

4.2 Volcanoes

Activity 1

Describe the features of a volcano

1 Using the diagram to help you, name the features of a volcano that match these descriptions.
   a The path which magma takes to travel up to the surface.
   b The hole in the ground where magma erupts.
   c A small volcanic hill on the side of the main volcano.
   d Liquid rock which comes out of the volcano.
2 Not all these features appear on the photograph of the volcano. Which of these features can you see on the photograph?
3 The diagram shows a model of a volcano. How does the model help you to understand how volcanoes form?

Think like a scientist

Draw a diagram of a volcano

Draw a diagram to show the internal structure of the volcano shown in the photograph. Label the parts.

How am I doing?

- Did I show the photograph of a volcano as a diagram?
- Did I add features to show the internal structure of the volcano?
- Did I label the features correctly?

How did you decide what to include on your diagram?

77

4 Earth and its habitats

Which parts of the world have volcanoes?

Some areas of the world have a high **risk** of a volcanic eruption. This is because there are many cracks in the Earth's crust in these areas. Magma can move up these cracks and erupt at the surface.

Other areas of the world have no cracks in the crust. These areas have a low risk of a volcanic eruption.

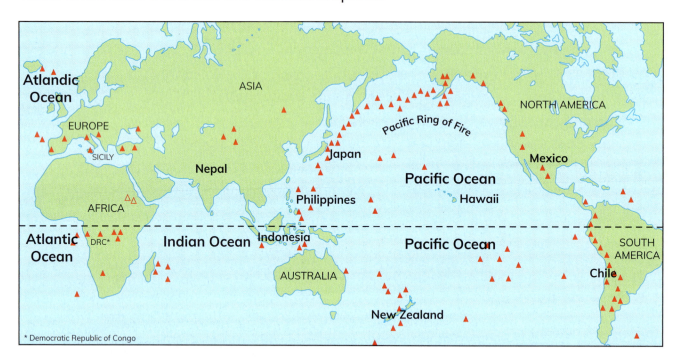

Activity 2

Describe where volcanoes erupt

Look at the map of the world, which shows where the main volcanoes are.

Questions

1. Around which ocean are there many volcanoes?
2. Trace with your finger along the volcanoes around this ocean. Name the countries as you go.
3. Why do you think this is called the Pacific Ring of Fire?
4. Find areas on the map that are unlikely to have volcanoes. Why are there no volcanoes here?

78

4.2 Volcanoes

> **Continued**
>
> 5 The country most at risk of having deadly volcanic eruptions is Indonesia. Look at the photograph of the damage left after a recent eruption there. The largest volcanic eruption was Mount Tamboura in Indonesia in 1812. This eruption killed 92 000 people. The Philippines and Japan also have a high risk of volcanoes.
>
> Find Indonesia, the Philippines and Japan on the map. Why do they have such a high risk of volcanoes?
>
>

Did you enjoy finding places on a map?
Did the map help you to see where most of the world's volcanoes are?

4 Earth and its habitats

How do volcanoes affect people?

You probably think that volcanoes only cause death and destruction! But millions of people live in volcanic regions. They know the risks. Volcanoes have positive as well as negative effects. Look at the drawing.

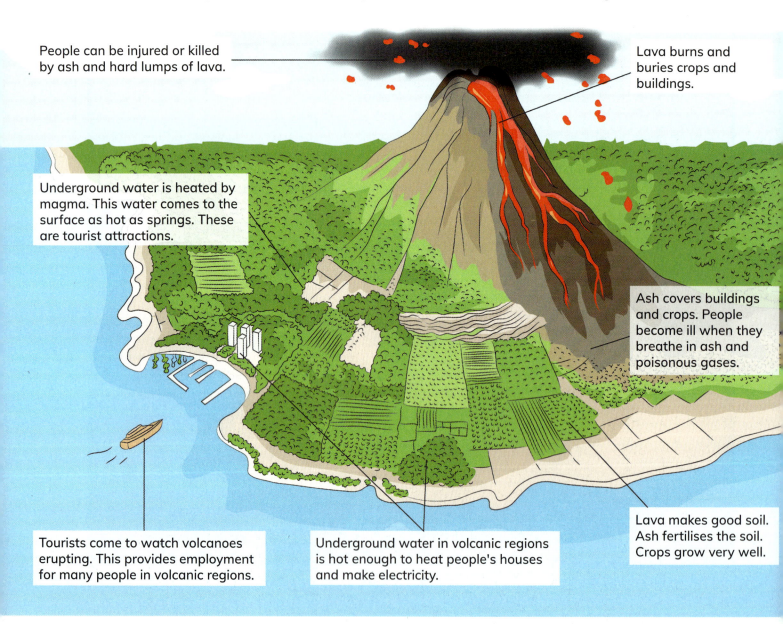

People can be injured or killed by ash and hard lumps of lava.

Lava burns and buries crops and buildings.

Underground water is heated by magma. This water comes to the surface as hot as springs. These are tourist attractions.

Ash covers buildings and crops. People become ill when they breathe in ash and poisonous gases.

Tourists come to watch volcanoes erupting. This provides employment for many people in volcanic regions.

Underground water in volcanic regions is hot enough to heat people's houses and make electricity.

Lava makes good soil. Ash fertilises the soil. Crops grow very well.

Question

Discuss which of the seven results of a volcanic eruption are positive effects and which are negative effects.

80

4.2 Volcanoes

Activity 3

What have I learnt about volcanoes?

Read about these two volcanoes.

Volcano A: Mount Etna, island of Sicily

Huge clouds of ash came out of Mount Etna's crater. Then jets of lava shot 100–200 metres into the air. The lava flowed down the sides of Mount Etna. It destroyed buildings and power lines in its path. Thousands of people had to leave their homes.

Volcano B: Goma, Democratic Republic of Congo

For three days lava poured out of a 500-metre-long crack and flowed through the town of Goma on the shore of Lake Kivu. Ash and gases poisoned the water in the lake. Forty-five people died from the poisonous gas. 500 000 people lost their homes. Lava spread halfway up their houses in a huge, flat layer.

Questions

1. Which volcano (A or B) is a composite volcano? How do you know this?
2. Which volcano is a volcanic plateau? How do you know this?
3. List the damage these two volcanoes caused.
4. Find Sicily on the world map. Why does Sicily often have volcanic eruptions?

Look what I can do!

- ☐ I can describe common features of volcanoes.
- ☐ I can use a model to help me understand how a volcano forms.
- ☐ I can draw a diagram to represent a real volcano.
- ☐ I can use a map to describe where volcanoes occur at breaks in the Earth's crust.

4 Earth and its habitats

> 4.3 Earthquakes

We are going to...
- find out that sudden movements of the Earth's crust can result in earthquakes
- use a model to see how an earthquake happens
- understand how an earthquake can result in a tsunami.

Getting started

Rub your hands together.
1. What movement are you making?
2. The movement creates energy. How do you feel this energy?

coastal area   landslide
earthquake   transfers
epicentre   tsunami
focus   wave

Earthquakes can cause terrible damage

In 2015 an **earthquake** hit Nepal. 'Quake' means shaking. So, an earthquake is a shaking of the Earth. More than 9000 people died and 23 000 people were injured. The first photograph shows the damage to buildings done by this earthquake. The second photograph shows damage to railway lines after an earthquake in Mexico in 2017.

The terrible damage in these photographs is caused by earthquakes.

82

4.3 Earthquakes

There are about 500 000 earthquakes each year around the world. Many of these earthquakes are so small that people don't notice them. But about 100 earthquakes a year are so strong that they cause damage like the scenes shown in the photographs. They also cause **landslides**, which are when soil and mud slide down slopes. The soil and mud can cover towns and crops.

How do earthquakes happen?

Earthquakes happen when there are sudden movements of rocks in the Earth's crust. The Earth's crust is made up of huge pieces of flat rock. Where two of these pieces meet, they rub together. This movement creates huge amounts of energy. The energy changes, or **transfers**, into **waves**. The waves travel through the crust to the Earth's surface. We feel these waves on the Earth's surface as an earthquake.

Look at the model of how an earthquake happens. The diagram shows a piece of the Earth's crust. The **focus** is where the earthquake begins inside the crust. Waves of energy pass through the crust and on to the surface. The worst damage at the surface is experienced immediately above the focus at a point called the **epicentre**.

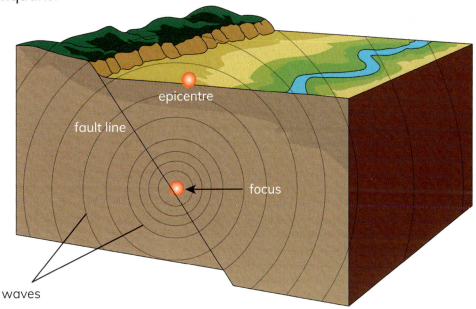

Which parts of the world are at risk of having earthquakes?

The parts of the world at risk of having earthquakes are the same areas that have a high risk of volcanoes. Both volcanoes and earthquakes happen where the rocks of the crust are broken and moving. Most earthquakes happen in the Pacific Ring of Fire.

4 Earth and its habitats

Activity 1

Find information about earthquakes

1 Describe the damage in the photograph of the Nepal earthquake.
2 Do you think the damage in the photograph was at the epicentre or the focus of the earthquake? Why?
3 Why do you think so many people died in the Nepal earthquake?
4 What has happened to the railway lines in the image of the Mexico City earthquake?
5 Find Nepal and Mexico on the world map in Topic 4.2. Which country is in the Pacific Ring of Fire?
6 What are the rocks in the crust below Nepal and Mexico doing to cause earthquakes?

How am I doing?

Give yourself ★ ★ ★ or ★ ★ or ★ for how well you can:

- Get information from a photograph
- Get information from a map.

Tsunamis

A **tsunami** is a huge sea wave. A tsunami happens when there is an earthquake or a volcanic eruption under the sea. The energy from the earthquake transfers to the sea to make huge waves. Sea waves increase in height when they reach shallow water. So when a tsunami reaches a shallow **coastal area**, the area along the border between the land and the sea, the wave can reach a height of 50 metres. This huge wave causes flooding of coastal areas.

Questions

This photograph shows what happened in Japan in 2011 when a tsunami hit the coast.

1 What is a tsunami?
2 What causes a tsunami?
3 Why did the tsunami increase in height when it reached the coast of Japan?
4 How do you think the boat got on top of the building?

84

4.3 Earthquakes

Activity 2

Case study: an earthquake in Chile

To finish this topic, here is a case study of an earthquake that happened in Chile. Read the case study and look at the map and the photographs. Then use your knowledge about earthquakes and tsunamis to help you to answer the questions.

A huge earthquake occurred off the coast of central Chile on Saturday 27 February 2010. The epicentre was just off the coast. Strong shaking lasted for about three minutes. Tremors were felt in Peru 2400 km further north.

The earthquake started a tsunami which destroyed several coastal towns in Chile. Tsunami warnings were sent to 53 countries, and the wave caused minor damage in California in the USA, and in Japan.

The earthquake caused a blackout that affected almost all the Chilean population and which went on for several days.

The President of Chile sent the army to take ontrol of the most affected areas. 525 people died, 25 people went missing and about 9% of the population lost their homes.

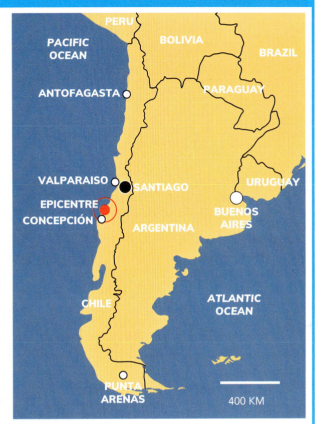

85

4 Earth and its habitats

> **Continued**
>
> **Questions**
>
> 1. a What is an epicentre?
>   b Where was the epicentre of the earthquake in Chile?
> 2. What is the focus of an earthquake?
> 3. Chile has had many earthquakes. Why does Chile have a high risk of earthquakes? (Look at Chile on the world map.)
> 4. List two types of damage you can see in the photographs.
> 5. Why do you think so many people died?
> 6. Why do you think Chile experienced blackouts for several days?
> 7. Why was the earthquake felt as far north as Peru?
> 8. Why did this earthquake start a tsunami?
> 9. Why were the effects of the tsunami felt in California and Japan?

Look what I can do!

☐ I can understand that an earthquake happens when there are sudden movements of rock in the Earth's crust.

☐ I can use a model to understand how an earthquake happens.

☐ I can recognise earthquake damage on photographs.

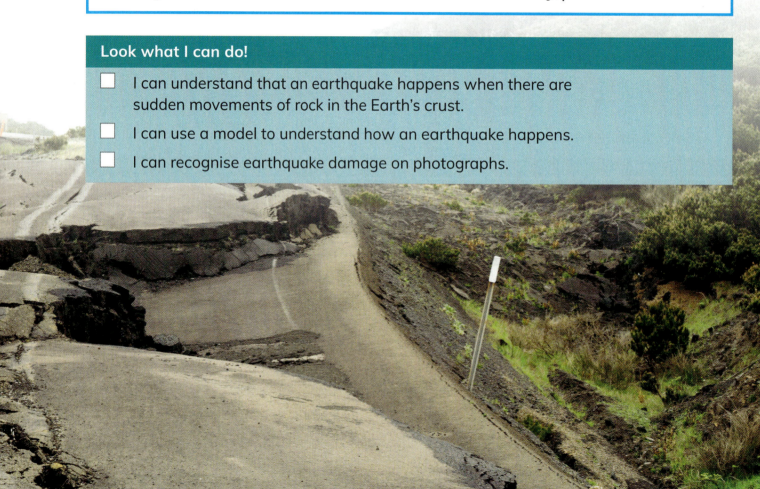

> 4.4 Different habitats

We are going to...

- see how different animals are suited to their habitat
- observe birds and how they are suited to their habitat
- see that repeating observations can give us more reliable data
- understand that animals and plants can survive in places that are not their normal habitat
- observe birds eating and classify them according to the shape of their beak
- present and interpret results on a dot plot.

Getting started

Look at the two habitats in the pictures.

1. Describe each habitat.
   Use the words 'hot', 'cold', 'dry', 'wet', 'lots of plants', 'few plants'.
2. Which habitat do you think has more animals and plants? Why?

beak   gills
crack open   strain
fins

87

4 Earth and its habitats

Animals are suited to their habitat

Animals live in a habitat which suits them. For example, fish have an organ called **gills**. Fish use gills to breathe underwater.

Fish also have **fins** which help them to swim.

Some types of fish live in warm water and other types of fish live in cold water. Sometimes water becomes warmer or colder because the climate changes. Fish manage to survive small changes like this as long as the changes happen slowly.

Questions

1. What do fish use to breathe underwater?
2. Why do fish sometimes have to move very fast? Which part of their bodies do they use to move fast?
3. Some people keep fish at home in a tank. This is not a normal habitat for a fish. Discuss how the fish survive.
4. If you buy a fish to keep in a tank at home, why is it important that you keep the fish in a bag of water until you can put it in the tank?

How are birds suited to their habitat?

Birds have wings which allow them to fly. But birds are suited to different habitats in other ways.

The habitat that a bird lives in affects what the bird eats. Birds which live near a river or sea habitat eat fish.

Birds that live in a grassland habitat eat seeds or insects. Other birds live in a habitat that has lots of trees. They eat fruits, seeds and small animals that live in the trees.

Birds have different sizes and shapes of **beaks**. These different beaks allow them to catch and eat different foods. Look at these examples:

- A pigeon eats mainly seeds. Look at its beak – it is small and pointed. A pigeon can **crack open** (break open) seeds with this beak.

88

4.4 Different habitats

- Starlings eat insects, worms and berries. A starling's beak is longer than a sparrow's beak because a starling eats bigger food. The pointed shape of the beak helps the starling to dig into the surface of the ground to get insects and worms.
- A kingfisher has a large beak with a sharp point. This helps them to catch fish in rivers.
- A flamingo's beak is very different to that of other birds. Flamingos eat small plants and animals in rivers and dams. A flamingo has a long, flat beak that can **strain** (sieve) these small plants and animals from the water.

starling

kingfisher

flamingo

89

4 Earth and its habitats

Activity 1

How birds are suited to different habitats

1 The table summarises how four different birds have beaks that help them eat food in their habitat. Copy and complete this table.

Bird	Shape of beak	How does the bird's beak help it to catch and eat food?
Pigeon	Small and _____	It _____ open seeds.
Kingfisher	Large with a sharp _____	It catches _____ .
Starling	_____ and pointed	It uses the point to _____ for worms.
Flamingo	Long and _____	It _____ plants and animals from water.

2 In towns and cities we can see birds in parks and gardens. There are often many different birds sharing a habitat. How do you think all the different birds survive?

3 Seagulls eat small fish and other animals in the sea. But they can survive inland. What do you think they eat to survive inland?

Think like a scientist

Bird watching

Work with a partner or work on your own.

> **You will need:**
> a field, a river, a garden or an open space where there are birds,
> a notebook and pencil to record your observations

- Observe the birds carefully. Don't frighten them away! Try to observe at least three different birds. If possible, take photographs.
- Identify the birds. Ask someone to help you identify the birds or look them up in a reference book.
- Answer these questions about each bird you observe:
  - What shape is the beak?
  - What is the bird eating?

4.4 Different habitats

Continued

- Make a drawing of the shape of each bird's beak.
- Describe the habitat the bird lives in – are there trees, water, grass, flowers? Is it hot, cold, dry or wet?
- Classify each bird as a seed eater, a fruit eater, a worm and insect eater, a fish eater or a water plant and animal eater.
- Repeat your observations on different days. Did this give you more reliable data about what the birds were eating?
- Record your observations in your notebook.
- Share your observations with the class.
- Draw a dot plot to present the numbers of each type of bird you saw. Label the x axis with the types of bird, e.g. seed eater, fruit eater. Look at the Skills section at the end of this book to find out how to draw a dot plot.

How am I doing?

- Were you patient enough when observing birds?
- Did you keep still and quiet?
- How could you have observed better?

Activity 2

How are tigers suited to their habitat?

Use what you have learnt in this topic to answer questions about how tigers are suited to their habitat. Read the information below and then answer the questions.

Tigers live in forests in parts of Asia. The tiger has a striped coat. The stripes help it blend in well with the sunlight that reaches the forest floor. The stripes also help break up the tiger's body shape. This makes it difficult for the smaller animals that tigers eat to see the tiger. There is not very much light in the forest but the tiger has very good hearing so it can hear other animals moving around.

4 Earth and its habitats

> **Continued**
>
> **Questions**
>
> 1. Describe the habitat the tiger lives in.
> 2. Explain two ways the tiger's coat makes it suited to its habitat.
> 3. Describe another way the tiger is suited to its habitat.
> 4. Tigers are kept in zoos. How do they survive in a zoo which is so different to their natural habitat?

Plants can also survive in places that are not their normal habitat

You have thought about some examples of animals that are surviving in places that are not their normal habitat, such as seagulls in a place far from the sea and fish in tanks.

What about plants? If you have a garden or you visit a park you will see many plants that are not in their natural habitat. For example, some plants may be suited to a wetter habitat. A gardener can water these plants so that they can survive in a habitat that is drier than their natural one.

Questions

1. Many people keep orchids in pots in their homes. The natural habitat of orchids is a hot, wet forest. How do orchids survive in pots in the home?
2. Bamboo is a fast-growing plant. Its natural habitat is a warm, wet climate in South East Asia. People all over the world plant bamboo in their gardens. How does the bamboo survive?
3. Think of plants you have growing at home. How do these plants survive?

> **Look what I can do!**
>
> ☐ I can see how different animals are suited to the habitats in which they are found.
> ☐ I can record observations in tables and drawings.
> ☐ I can see that repeating observations can give more reliable data.
> ☐ I realise that plants and animals can survive in places other than their habitats.
> ☐ I can present and interpret my bird observations on a dot plot.

Project: How people use volcanoes and hot springs

Project: How people use volcanoes and hot springs

In this unit you have found out about the structure of the Earth and volcanoes. You know that it gets hotter as you go deeper into the crust. We see evidence of this when lava erupts at the surface in a volcano. We also see this when water from deep in the crust reaches the surface as a hot spring. People make use of these things. They can use the hot water in their homes or make the hot springs into a tourist attraction. Volcanoes are also tourist attractions. Many people choose to live on the sides of a volcano because the soil is rich and crops grow well.

- Find out how people make use of a hot spring or a volcano in your country. If there isn't one in your country choose one in another country.
- Name the volcano or hot spring and describe where it is. You can draw a map to show this. Describe how it used by people.
- Present your project as a poster. Illustrate with photographs or drawings or pictures cut out of magazines.
- Use colours and pictures to make your poster eye-catching.
- Remember to give your poster a heading.

93

4 Earth and its habitats

Check your progress

1 Match up the words 1–8 with their meanings A–H.

Word	Meaning
1 Crust	A A shaking of the Earth
2 Crater	B A place where a plant or animal lives
3 Internal structure	C A large hole at the top of a volcano where material erupts
4 Earthquake	D The outer layer of the Earth, formed of rocks
5 Habitat	E A huge sea wave caused by an earthquake that starts under the sea
6 Core	F The layer of the Earth below the crust
7 Tsunami	G The centre of the Earth
8 Mantle	H Materials that make up the inside of the Earth

2 Look at the diagram.

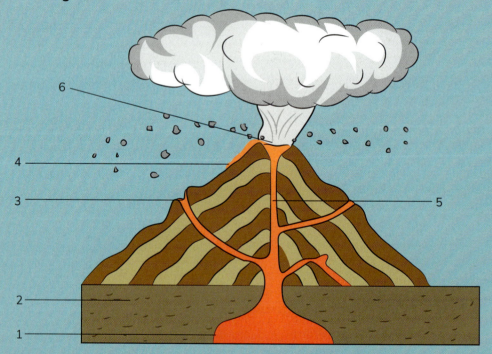

a   What does this diagram represent?

b   Label the parts 1–6 on the diagram beside the numbers.

94

Check your progress

Continued

3 Look at this photograph of damage caused by an earthquake.

   a The town in the photograph was near the epicentre of the earthquake. What is the epicentre?

   b What causes an earthquake to happen?

4 Look at the photograph of an African sunbird. These birds feed on the sugary nectar deep inside flowers.

   a Describe the sunbird's beak.
   b Describe how the sunbird's beak helps it to live in its habitat.
   c If the sunbird was forced to live in a habitat without these flowers, how could it survive?
   d The flower in the photograph is on a bush called a protea. The natural habitat of these bushes is in the mountains at the south-western tip of South Africa. The soil is sandy and it is dry and sunny in summer. Winters are wet and windy. But people grow proteas in different habitats. How do you think the proteas survive?

5 Light

> 5.1 How we see things

We are going to...

- investigate how we see things that are not sources of light
- make predictions and see if results support our predictions
- make a conclusion from our results.

> reflect   source

Getting started

1. Identify the **sources** of light in the pictures – where does the light come from?

2. What is the source of light in your classroom?
3. How do you think you are able to see your teacher?

5.1 How we see things

How do we see things that are not sources of light?

Let's investigate this question.

> **Think like a scientist**
>
> **Investigate how we see an object**
>
> > **You will need:**
> > a large cardboard box with lid, a flashlight with batteries, a small object such as a coin, a pen knife or craft knife
>
> **Be careful when you use the knife.**
>
> - Cut two holes in the lid of the box as shown in the picture. One hole must be big enough for your flashlight to fit through and the other hole must be big enough for you to see through. Place the coin on the bottom of the box. Replace the lid on the box.
> - Cover the flashlight hole with your hand. Predict whether you will be able to see the coin when you look through the other hole.
> - Test your prediction.
> - Shine your flashlight though the flashlight hole. Predict whether you will be able to see the coin now when you look through the other hole.
> - Test your prediction.
>
>

5 Light

Continued

Questions

1. Can you see the coin without shining the flashlight?
2. Can you see the coin when you shine the flashlight?
3. What conclusion do you reach about the question:
   How do we see things that are not sources of light?
   Copy and complete these sentences to help you write your conclusion:

Light travels from the ____ source (the flashlight) to the object (the ____). The light bounces or **reflects** off the ____ into our ____. This is how I can see the object.

How am I doing?

How well can I:	Very well 😊	Quite well 😐	I need help 😟
make a prediction?			
test a prediction?			
make a conclusion?			

Activity

How can the person see the car?
Look at the picture.

Questions

1. Identify the source of light.
2. Identify the object.
3. Write a sentence to explain how the person can see the car.
4. Discuss in class how the person could see the car at night.

Look what I can do!

- ☐ I can understand that I see an object because light reflects off the object into my eyes.
- ☐ I can make a prediction and see if results support my predictions.
- ☐ I can make a conclusion based on an investigation.

> 5.2 Light travels in straight lines

We are going to...

- investigate how light travels
- make a prediction and see if results support our prediction
- make a conclusion from the results
- draw a ray diagram.

Getting started

1. Name the source of light in the photographs on this page and the next page.
2. Describe how the light in these photographs travels – in a curved line or a straight line?
3. Can light travel round corners?

proof   ray

prove   ray diagram

5 Light

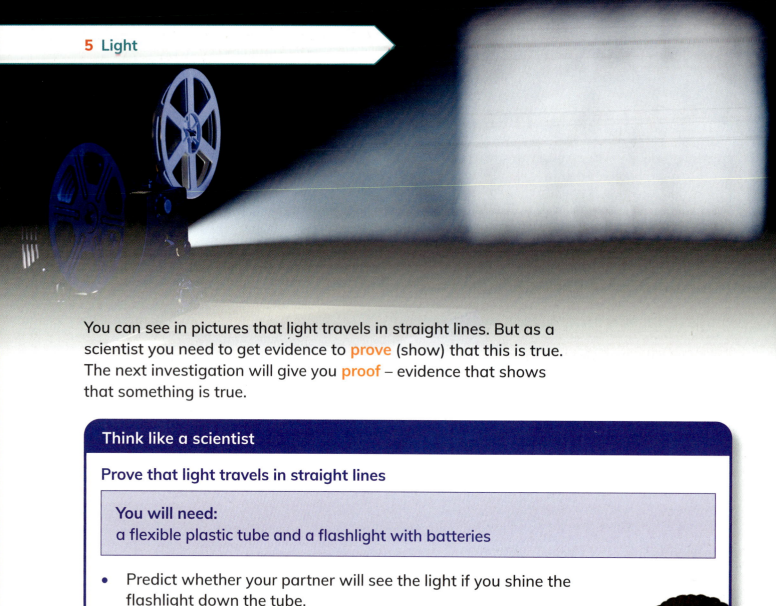

You can see in pictures that light travels in straight lines. But as a scientist you need to get evidence to **prove** (show) that this is true. The next investigation will give you **proof** – evidence that shows that something is true.

Think like a scientist

Prove that light travels in straight lines

> **You will need:**
> a flexible plastic tube and a flashlight with batteries

- Predict whether your partner will see the light if you shine the flashlight down the tube.
- Shine your flashlight down the plastic tube.
- Can your partner see the light when they look down the other end of the tube?
- Make a bend in the tube.
- Predict whether your partner will see the light if you shine the flashlight down the bent tube.
- Shine your flashlight down the tube again.
- Now can your partner see the light when they look down the other end?
- What do you conclude about how light travels?'

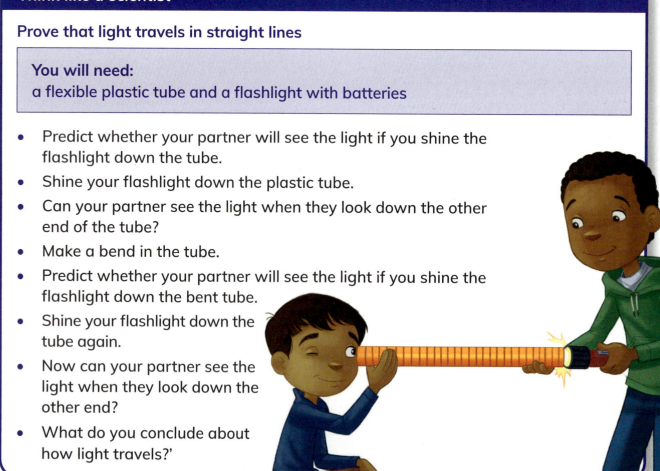

5.2 Light travels in straight lines

Light rays

Look again at the photographs of light travelling from the Sun and the film projector.

In both photographs you can see the light is travelling in straight lines. Each narrow beam of light is called a **ray**. Light rays travel from the source of light in all directions until they hit something.

Ray diagrams

We can show how light travels with a **ray diagram**. On the diagram, we draw straight lines for the rays of light. We draw an arrowhead to show the direction the light ray is moving. Here is an example of a ray diagram with light rays travelling from a lamp.

Imagine a light ray from the lamp hits an object such as a book. This light ray is an arriving ray. The light rays will bounce or reflect off the book. These rays are called reflected rays. The reflected rays are also straight lines but they travel in a different direction to the rays leaving the light source. If the reflected rays enter our eyes we will see the book. Here is a ray diagram to show this.

Let's revisit the coin in the box. We can show how light travels using a ray diagram.

5 Light

Activity

Practise drawing ray diagrams

1. In the ray diagram of the coin in the box, which is the reflected ray, A or B?
2. Look at the ray diagram of the person seeing the car. Identify the arriving ray and the reflected ray labelled 1 and 2.
3. Draw a ray diagram to show how you see the person sitting next to you. Label the arriving ray and the reflected ray.

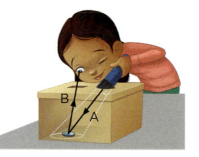

How am I doing?

How well can I:	Very well 🙂	Quite well 😐	I need help ☹
identify the arriving ray and the reflected ray on a ray diagram?			
draw a ray diagram?			

Look what I can do!

☐ I can understand that light travels from a source in straight lines called rays.

☐ I can predict what will happen before doing an investigation and then compare results with predictions.

☐ I can label rays on a ray diagram and draw a ray diagram to show how light travels.

☐ I can make a conclusion about how light travels.

> 5.3 Light reflects off different surfaces

> **We are going to…**
> - look at examples of how well a mirror reflects light
> - Investigate how well light reflects off different surfaces
> - make predictions and see if results support our predictions
> - describe simple patterns in results and make a conclusion.

> **Getting started**
> 1. Why can't we see things in a completely dark room?
> 2. Discuss how you can see the person sitting next to you.

absorb   image   mirror   reflection   surface

You know that when light reflects off an object into our eyes we see the object. Some **surfaces** – the top layer that is next to the air – are much better at reflecting light than other surfaces.

Mirrors

A smooth, shiny surface is very good at reflecting light. A **mirror** has a smooth, shiny surface. When you see your face in a mirror you are seeing light from your face reflecting off the mirror. We call the **reflection** of your face in the mirror your **image**.

103

5 Light

Where have you got mirrors at home? What do you use the mirrors for?

Look at the pictures on this page. The pictures show different ways people use mirrors. Discuss how these mirrors help people to see objects they couldn't see without the mirror.

Activity

Describe how people use mirrors to see things

Discuss the answers to these questions.

1. Imagine you are riding the bike in the photo. Describe the way the light travels when you see a bike behind you in the rear view mirror.
2. How does the mirror in the shop help the shop manager?
3. How does the mirror help the dentist to see the patient's teeth?

5.3 Light reflects off different surfaces

Do some surfaces reflect light better than others?

Arun can see himself in the mirror. The mirror reflects his image back to him. Marcus can't see himself in the wooden chopping board. The wooden surface **absorbs** light. It takes the light in and does not reflect it.

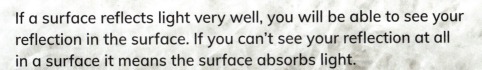

All objects reflect light or absorb light. A piece of paper, for example, is smooth and flat. However, if you looked at a piece of paper under a microscope, you'd see something like the picture below. Notice that the paper actually contains lots of bumps. The microscope makes everything bigger and you can see the bumps that you can't see with your eyes. Because its surface is not completely smooth, paper absorbs a lot more light than it reflects.

If a surface reflects light very well, you will be able to see your reflection in the surface. If you can't see your reflection at all in a surface it means the surface absorbs light.

A piece of paper as seen under a microscope

5 Light

Think like a scientist

Investigate how well different surfaces reflect light

You will need:
At least six objects with different surfaces.
Look at the picture to see some examples.

- Your teacher will set up objects you are using for your investigation.
- Predict which surfaces you think will reflect light well. List your surfaces beginning with the surface you think will reflect light best.
- To test each material ask the question: How well can I see my reflection in the surface of the material? Use this scale:

  3: Perfect reflection

  2: Fairly good reflection

  1: Poor reflection

  0: No reflection
- See if your prediction was correct

Questions

1. How well did your results support your predictions?
2. What pattern did you notice in your results?
3. What conclusion can you make from your investigation?
4. Identify which of the five types of scientific enquiry you have just done. Choose from

    1. Research
    2. Fair testing
    3. Observing over time
    4. Identifying and classifying
    5. Pattern seeking

5.3 Light reflects off different surfaces

Continued

How am I doing?

How well can I:	Very well 🙂	Quite well 😐	I need help ☹
make a prediction?			
test a prediction?			
make a conclusion?			

Do you think you have improved since the last assessment?

Did you enjoy this topic?

How did the 'Think like a scientist' investigation help you to learn today?

Look what I can do!

☐ I can see that a mirror reflects light very well.
☐ I can investigate how well light reflects off different surfaces.
☐ I can make predictions and see if results support my predictions.
☐ I can describe a pattern in results and make a conclusion.

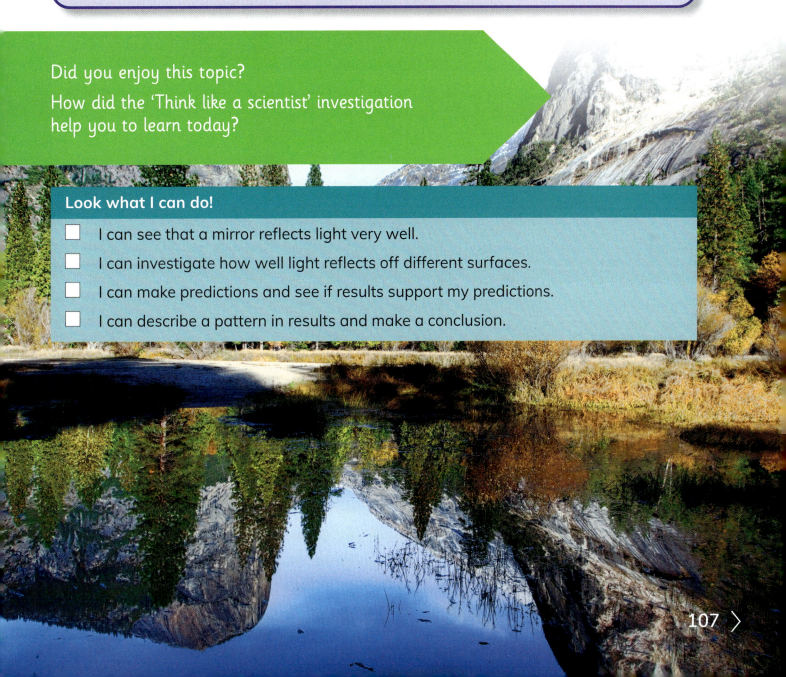

107

5 Light

> 5.4 Light in the solar system

We are going to...

- discover that solar systems can contain stars, planets, asteroids and comets
- name the planets in our solar system
- draw a diagram of a moon orbiting a planet
- use a model to show the relationship between bodies in the solar system
- use reference books and the internet to find out more about the solar system.

Getting started

1   Which is the Sun, the Earth and the Moon in this photo?
2   Which of these is a star and which is a planet?
3   What is the difference between a star and a planet?

asteroid   orbit
closest   solar system
comet   spacecraft
furthest

5.4 Light in the solar system

The Sun is our source of light

The **spacecraft** Galileo took this photograph of the Earth and the Moon on its way to explore the planet Jupiter. The photograph shows us that the Moon and the Earth are surrounded by black, empty space. The Sun is way beyond the photograph on the left. The Sun is shining because it is a star. The Sun lights up the half of the Earth and the Moon facing it. Earth is a planet. Planets reflect the light of the Sun. The Moon also reflects the light of the Sun.

Orbits

Look at the diagram of the Sun, Earth and Moon.
The Earth and the Moon are constantly moving in space.

The Moon **orbits** – goes around – the Earth and the Earth orbits the Sun.
The Moon takes 29 days or one month to complete its orbit around the Earth.
The Earth takes $365\frac{1}{4}$ days or one year to complete its orbit around the Sun.

In space there are many stars. Each of these stars gives out light. That is why we can see the stars in the night sky. Light from the stars travels to Earth and enters our eyes. Many of the stars could have planets orbiting them in the same way as planets orbit the Sun.

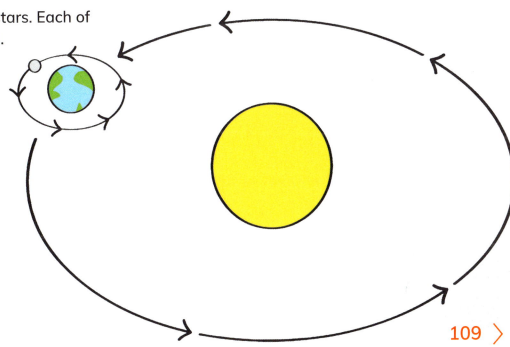

5 Light

Our solar system

The solar system – which means the Sun and the planets, moons, comets and asteroids which move around it – is enormous. We can learn about the solar system by using a model. The diagram of the solar system shown here is a model. All the distances and sizes are much smaller than the real thing.

The Sun is at the centre of the solar system. There are eight planets which orbit the Sun. Earth is one of the planets.

Notice that the planets that are closest, or nearest, to the Sun have smaller orbits than the planets further from the Sun. Planets that are closer to the Sun than Earth take less than an 'Earth year' to orbit the Sun. Planets that are further from the Sun than Earth take more than an 'Earth year' to orbit the Sun.

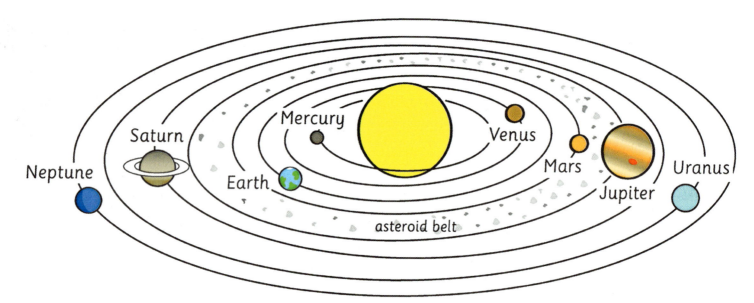

5.4 Light in the solar system

> **Activity**
>
> **Planets in our solar system**
>
> Use the diagram of the solar system to find the answers to these questions.
>
> 1 What body is at the centre of our solar system?
>   Why is this body so important to us?
> 2 List the planets in our solar system in order from the one closest to the Sun to the one **furthest** – the most far away – from the Sun.
> 3 Here are the times it takes two planets to orbit the Sun:
>   A: 88 Earth days. B: 29.5 Earth years.
>   a Which planet, A or B, is Saturn? Explain why.
>   b Which planet, A or B, is Mercury? Explain why.

There are also many asteroids, moons and comets in the solar system.

Asteroids

Asteroids are rocky masses that orbit the Sun. They are similar to planets but much smaller. At the moment scientists have identified 781 692 asteroids! Nearly all of them are in the asteroid belt between the planets Mars and Jupiter.

Moons

Moons orbit planets and asteroids. Earth has one moon. Mars has two moons. This photograph shows Titania. It is the largest of the moons of planet Uranus and the eighth largest moon in the solar system.

5 Light

Questions

1 What is an asteroid?
2 Where are most of the asteroids in the solar system?
3 What is a moon?
4 In the photograph of Titania, why is half the moon in darkness?
5 Draw a diagram to show the orbit Titania makes around planet Uranus.
6 Use a reference book or the internet to find out how many moons the planet Jupiter has. You will be surprised!

Comets

Comets are lumps of ice and dirt which move in large orbits around the Sun.
Many comets are beyond the planets at the edge of the solar system.
Comets have long tails behind them.

Think like a scientist

Find out what is in our solar system

1 What other bodies orbit a star besides planets?
2 Name two types of body that a moon can orbit.
3 Draw a ray diagram of the Sun's rays travelling to Earth
4 Find out:
   a how many moons planet Saturn has
   b the name of Saturn's largest moon.
5 Find out the name of the biggest asteroid in our solar system.

Look what I can do!

☐ I can show that the Sun is the centre of our solar system.

☐ I can name the planets in our solar system.

☐ I can describe the contents of solar systems as stars, planets, asteroids and comets.

☐ I can use a model to show relationships between bodies in the solar system.

☐ I can draw a diagram of a moon orbiting a planet.

☐ I can use reference books and the internet to find out more about the solar system.

> 5.5 Day and night

We are going to...

- explain what causes night and day
- use a globe as a model to show night and day
- complete and label a diagram.

Getting started

1. Where does the Sun rise in the morning?
2. Where does the Sun set in the evening?
3. The Sun appears to move across the sky during the day. Does the Sun really move?

anticlockwise   spin
axis   tilted
globe

A model of the Earth

The globe is a model of the Earth. It is shaped like a ball and it has a stick passing through it from the North Pole to the South Pole. This stick represents the Earth's axis. In space, the Earth is not upright. The Earth leans over, or tilts. The Earth is tilted on an imaginary axis like the globe.

The Earth spins

The Earth turns round and round or spins all the time on its axis. If you look at the top of the Earth – that is, the North Pole – the Earth spins in an anticlockwise direction. This is the opposite way to the hands on a clock.

The Earth does one complete turn on its axis every 24 hours.

113

5 Light

Find your country on the globe. Put a piece of sticky tape on your country. Now spin the globe on its axis and watch your country go round and round. This movement happens all the time but we do not notice it.

Imagine driving very fast. You are travelling at 120 mph, which seems fast. But Earth is spinning on its axis at least ten times faster than this!

In the next investigation you will see how spinning causes day and night.

Think like a scientist

Use a model to show day and night

You will need: a globe, a sticker, a flashlight

- In your model the flashlight represents the Sun and the globe represents the Earth. Shine the flashlight on the globe. This represents the Sun shining on the Earth. Now spin the globe in an anticlockwise direction.
- Observe which part of the model Earth is lit up. Can the whole Earth be lit up at one time?
- Now stick a sticker on the Earth. Continue to shine the flashlight on the Earth. Spin the Earth and watch the sticker.
- Is the sticker lit up by the flashlight all the time? As the Earth spins, say 'day' when the light shines on the sticker and 'night' when no light shines on the sticker.

5.5 Day and night

Continued

Questions

1 Copy and complete this sentence:

   The Earth _____ on its axis once every 24 hours.
   This movement causes _____ and _____.

2

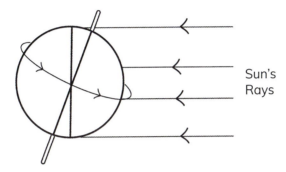

Sun's Rays

   Copy the diagram. Find the half of the Earth having night and colour it black. Find the half of the Earth having day and colour it yellow.

3 Ali lives in Malaysia. Farouk lives in Spain. If Ali wants to contact Farouk he should phone when it is evening in Malaysia. Why shouldn't he phone Farouk when it is lunchtime in Malaysia?

4 What would it be like if the Earth completed one rotation every 10 hours?

How am I doing?

- Explain the idea of night and day to a younger person such as a younger brother or sister.
- Plan how you could explain night and day with a model using objects at home.

Look what I can do!

☐ I can use a globe as a model to show night and day.

☐ I can understand that the Earth's spinning on its axis causes night and day.

☐ I can complete and label a diagram to show day and night.

115

5 Light

> 5.6 Investigating shadow lengths

We are going to...

- explain changes in shadows in terms of Earth spinning on its axis
- make predictions and identify if results support our predictions
- measure the lengths of shadows and describe simple patterns in results
- repeat measurements to get more reliable data
- make a conclusion from results.

apparent movement

Getting started

1. What is the source of light in this picture?
2. What is blocking the light?
3. What results from blocking the light?

116

5.6 Investigating shadow lengths

Shadow lengths

Look at these two pictures of a golf flag.

Questions

1. What causes the shadows?
2. What is the difference between the two shadows?
3. Which shadow do you think was formed at midday and which shadow was formed in the late afternoon?
4. Why do you think the shadows are different at different times of day?

In the next task you will investigate how shadows change in length and direction throughout the day.

Think like a scientist

Investigate the changing length and position of a shadow

> You will need:
> a sunny day, a stick about 20 cm high, a sheet of white paper, some modelling clay, four stones, a ruler, a marker pen

- Choose a place in full sunlight (where there are no shadows nearby) to set up your stick. Push the stick into the ground or position it upright with modelling clay.
- Set up your paper and stick like this at 09:00.

Make sure you do not look directly at the Sun as you may damage your eyes.

5 Light

Continued

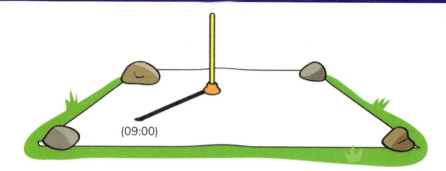

- You will see that a shadow of the stick falls on the paper. Mark the end of the shadow on the paper with a marker pen. Write the time.
- Go outside every hour and mark the end of the shadow and then write the time.
- Also observe where the Sun is in the sky each time. Does the Sun appear to move from one part of the sky to another?
- Think about whether this is really what is happening. Is there another explanation for the way the Sun seems to move – its **apparent movement**? Think back to what you learnt in the last topic.
- At the end of the afternoon take the stick down and bring the paper inside.

Here is the shadow stick paper used by Aleisha and her friends:

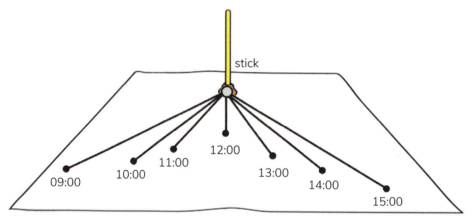

- Join the dots you made for the ends of the shadows to the hole where the stick was. These are your shadow lines. Measure the length of each shadow line with a ruler. Record the lengths of the shadows in a table alongside the times.
- If it was cloudy on the first day, repeat this experiment over several days, using a different sheet of paper each day. In this way you will get a more complete and, therefore, more reliable set of shadow lengths.

5.6 Investigating shadow lengths

Continued

Questions

1 Draw a picture of the shadows you recorded. Show how the length and direction of the shadows changed. Label the times.
2 What did you notice about the position of the Sun at different times of day?
   a Was the Sun low in the sky or high in the sky? How did this affect the length of the shadow?
   b Did the Sun appear to move from one side to the other? How did this affect the position of the shadow at different times of day?
3 What pattern did you notice about the length of the shadow and the time of day?
4 What pattern did you notice about the position of the shadow at different times of day?
5 Did you find that on different days you were able to observe shadows that you had not been able to observe on other days? Why was this?
6 Use what you learnt in the previous topic to explain the apparent movement of the Sun at different times of day.

How am I doing?

Answer 'Very well', 'Quite well' or 'I need more practice' to these questions:

- How well can I describe a pattern in results?
- How well can I give a scientific explanation for a pattern in results?

What did you learn about the Sun's changing shadows?
What did you find easy? What did you find difficult?

Look what I can do!

- ☐ I can make predictions before carrying out an investigation and see whether my predictions are correct or not.
- ☐ I can describe patterns in results.
- ☐ I can see that repeating the measurements on different days gives more reliable data.
- ☐ I can explain changes in shadows in the shadow stick investigation using science knowledge.

5 Light

Project: Research the life and discoveries of an astronomer

For thousands of years scientists have studied space. Six of these scientists are mentioned in the information below. Choose one of the scientists mentioned below or a different scientist. Use library books or the internet to find out more about the scientist's life and discoveries. Find out how the scientist you chose discovered new information about the solar system.

Use these headings to organise your information:

- Name of scientist
- Date of birth and death
- Nationality
- What did they discover?
- What equipment did they use?
- How did they change ideas about the solar system?

Work with a partner to make a short presentation to the rest of the class.

How scientists discovered the solar system

Scientists who study space are called astronomers. Two thousand years ago people believed that the Earth was flat and that the Earth was at the centre of the solar system. An Egyptian astronomer called Ptolemy described how the Moon, Sun, planets and stars revolved around Earth.

The Indian astronomers Varahamihira and Bramagupta suggested that the Earth and the planets were round and not flat.

About 1500 years ago, the astronomer Aryabhata agreed that the Earth was round. He stated that the apparent rotation of the planets was a result of the actual rotation of the Earth.

Five hundred years ago a Polish astronomer, Copernicus, observed the movements of the planets and decided that the previous astronomers were wrong. He wrote a book saying that the Earth and all other planets moved around the Sun. For a long time nobody believed him!

Four hundred years ago the Italian astronomer Galileo studied the sky. A picture of Galileo is shown above. He used the newly invented telescope to do this. He noticed that the planet Venus had different sides lit up by the Sun at different times. This means that Venus must move around the Sun. Galileo agreed with Copernicus.

Check your progress

Check your progress

1 Match words A–G with their meanings, 1–7.

A	Reflect
B	Ray
C	Ray
D	Proof
E	Spin
F	Comet
G	Comet

1	A line that light travels in
2	A lump of ice and dirt that travels in a large orbit around the Sun
3	Scientific evidence that something is true
4	Go round and round very fast
5	The action of light bouncing off a surface
6	In the opposite direction to a clock's hands
7	Rocky masses that orbit the Sun

2 Which surfaces from the list below reflect light and which surfaces absorb light?

muddy water   mirror   clear water   wood

3 a Write the labels for the features numbered 1–5 on the diagram.

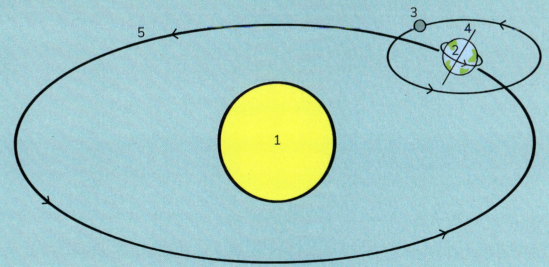

b What does the Earth do to cause day and night?

c List the planets besides Earth that orbit the Sun.

5 Light

Continued

4 Look at the picture showing Rachel finding her cat.

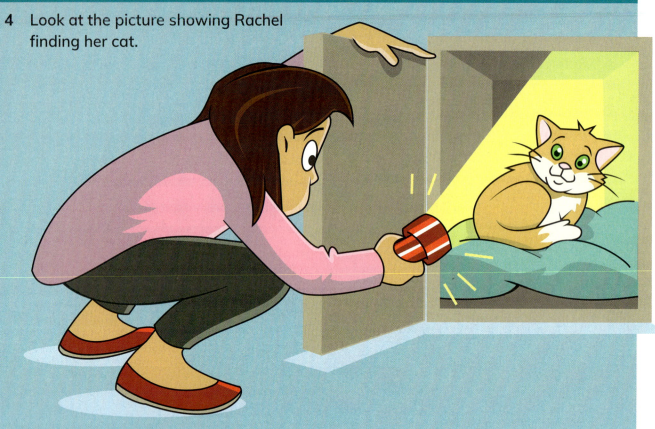

   a Identify the light source.

   b Identify the object.

   c Draw a simple ray diagram to show how Rachel sees the cat.

5 Some children did a shadow stick experiment. Read these sentences about shadow length at different times of the day. Choose and write down the correct alternatives.

   a Between 08:00 and midday the shadow becomes **shorter / longer**.

   b Between midday and 16:00 the shadow becomes **shorter / longer**.

   c The shadow is **longest / shortest** at sunrise and sunset.

   d The shadow is **longest / shortest** in the middle of the day.

   e The changes in shadow length are because **the Earth spins on its axis / the Sun moves across the sky**.

Check your progress

Continued

6 Emilio and Julio are travelling by car through a tunnel. The tunnel is 10 km long. At first it is completely dark in the tunnel. Then, after five minutes Julio says, 'Look I can see the light at the end of the tunnel!'

Explain why the boys could not see the light at the end of the tunnel to begin with.

6 Electricity

> 6.1 Which materials conduct electricity?

We are going to...

- use a fair test to group objects into conductors and insulators of electricity
- identify risks and carry out practical work safely
- make predictions and identify if results support predictions or do not support predictions
- describe simple patterns in results and make a conclusion from results.

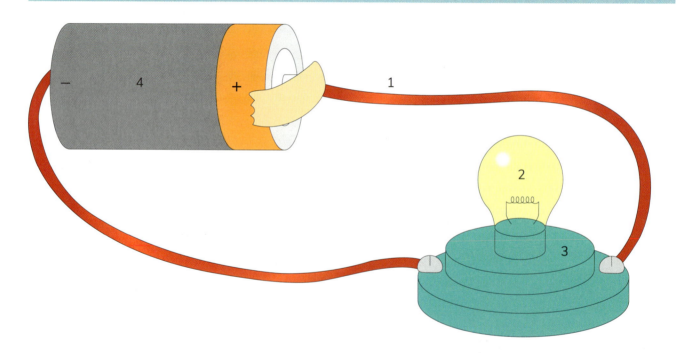

Getting started

1. Name the components of the circuit numbered 1, 2, 3 and 4.
2. What is the function of the component 4?
3. Why does the lamp light up in this circuit?

conductor   insulator

6.1 Which materials conduct electricity?

Conductors and insulators

A material that allows electricity to pass through it is called a conductor.

A material that does not allow electricity to pass through it is called an insulator.

In the next investigation you are going to test different materials to see whether they are conductors or insulators.

> **Think like a scientist**
>
> **Test which materials conduct electricity**
>
> **You will need:**
> one piece of plastic-covered wire with a crocodile clip on one end, a screwdriver, a 1.5 V cell in a cell holder with a crocodile clip on the end of one of the wires, a 1.5 V lamp in a lamp holder, objects made of different materials
>
> **Before you begin, make sure you follow safety rules:**
>
> - If you have to cut the plastic off the ends of the wires, use a wire stripper. Grip the wire in your left hand and strip off the plastic away from you.
> - When the circuit is complete, do not touch any bare electric wires. Always hold the plastic covered wire.
>
> **Questions**
>
> 1. Why is it important to cut away from you?
> 2. How can you strip the plastic off the wires safely?
> 3. Why must you not touch bare wires when the circuit is complete?
>
> **Step 1**
>
> - Attach the end of wire from the cell holder which doesn't have a crocodile clip to one side of the lamp holder.
> - Use the screwdriver to loosen the screw of lamp holder and then tighten it after you have wound the wire around. Use tape to attach wires to the cell.
>
> Attach the separate piece of wire to the other side of the lamp holder. Again, attach the end which doesn't have a crocodile clip to the lamp.

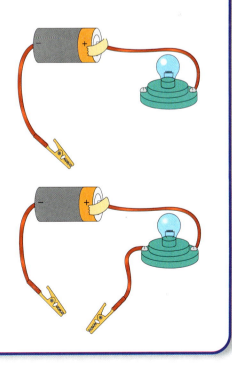

6 Electricity

> **Continued**
>
> **Step 2**
>
>
>
> - Check that your circuit works. Hold the wires and clips where they are covered in plastic. Allow the crocodile clips to touch.
> - If the lamp lights up, the circuit is complete. If the lamp does not light up there is a break in the circuit. Check that you have connected the wires properly.
> - If you separate the crocodile clips, you break the circuit and the lamp goes out. This is your testing equipment. You will use the same testing equipment to see which materials allow electricity to pass through.
> - Before you begin, predict which materials will allow electricity to pass through and which will not. Record your predictions in a table like the one below. Place a tick ✓ in the 2nd or 3rd column.
>
> | Material | Prediction | | Result | |
> |---|---|---|---|---|
> | | conductor | insulator | conductor | insulator |
> | | | | | |
> | | | | | |
> | | | | | |
> | | | | | |
> | | | | | |
> | | | | | |
>
> **Step 3**
>
> - Test each material. Hold one crocodile clip at one end of the object. Hold the second crocodile clip at the other end of the object.
> - If the lamp does not light up you can try again to make sure.
> - Record your results by placing ticks ✓ in the last two columns of your table.

6.1 Which materials conduct electricity?

> **Continued**
>
> **Questions**
>
> 4 How well did your results support your predictions?
>
> 5 How did you make sure that the test was fair?
>
> 6 Identify a pattern of which types of material are conductors and which are insulators.
>
> 7 Did any materials not fit this pattern? If so, identify the material.
>
> 8 What conclusion can you make from your results?
>
> 9 Which two types of scientific enquiry have you practised in this activity?
>
> 10 Why are lightning conductors made from copper?
>
> **How am I doing?**
>
> How many stars (★, ★★ or ★★★) would you give yourself for these skills?
>
> - Can I identify and describe a pattern in results?
> - Can I make a conclusion from results that answer the question?

What have you learnt about working safely with electricity?

> **Look what I can do!**
>
> ☐ I can predict which materials will be conductors and insulators of electricity.
>
> ☐ I can use a circuit to make a fair test to group materials into conductors and insulators of electricity and test my predictions.
>
> ☐ I can know the risks and work safely doing practical work.
>
> ☐ I can identify a pattern in results.
>
> ☐ I can make a conclusion from results.

6 Electricity

> 6.2 Does water conduct electricity?

We are going to...

- investigate if water conducts electricity
- identify and explain risks and carry out practical work safely
- make predictions and identify if results support predictions or do not support predictions
- make a conclusion from results
- identify the risks and carry out practical work safely.

distilled water

pure water

Getting started

1. If we put salt into water and stir it, what happens to the salt?
2. How can we test to see if a material conducts electricity or not?

Is water pure?

Water from a river or the tap is not pure water. It has salts dissolved in it. Distilled water is pure water. Distilled water is water that has been boiled and the steam has been allowed to cool down to form liquid water again. This water is distilled water and contains no salts.

All living things contain water. Our bodies are about 65% water! This water has salts dissolved in it so it is not pure.

6.2 Does water conduct electricity?

Think like a scientist

Investigate whether water conducts electricity

> **You will need:**
> a circuit with two 1.5 V cells in a cell holder, a piece of plastic-coated wire, distilled water, a beaker, two teaspoons of salt, aluminium foil

Your teacher will show you this investigation.

- Connect the circuit with the cells, the lamp in the lamp holder and one length of wire.
- Test the circuit by holding the crocodile clips together. Does the lamp light up?
- Fold two pieces of aluminium foil and put them into the crocodile clips at the end of each wire. This gives a larger surface in contact with the water.
- Pour 250 ml of distilled water into the beaker. Dip the aluminium foil ends into the water.
- Predict whether the lamp will light up.
- Observe whether the lamp lights up.
- Remove the aluminium foil ends from the water.
- Add two teaspoons of salt to the water and stir it. Now dip the aluminium foil ends into the salt water. Predict whether the lamp will light up.
- Observe whether the lamp lights up.

Aluminium foil connected to a crocodile clip

G Electricity

Continued

Questions

1. Did your results support your predictions or not?
2. Compare the results you got with pure water and with salty water.
3. What conclusion can you make about whether water conducts electricity?
4. Would your body be a good or a bad conductor of electricity? Explain why.
5. Use your answer to question 4 to explain why it is not safe to touch the bare wires when the circuit is closed.
6. Why is it dangerous to swim in the sea when there is a thunderstorm with lightning?

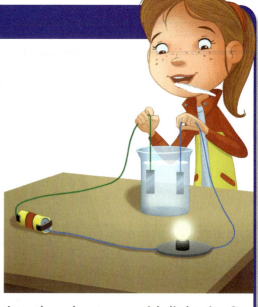

6.2 Does water conduct electricity?

Did you enjoy the demonstration?

Did it help you to learn about conductors and insulators?

Were you surprised to learn that your body is a conductor of electricity?

Look what I can do!

- [ ] I can investigate if water conducts electricity.
- [ ] I can make predictions and identify if results support predictions or not.
- [ ] I know the risks and can carry out practical work safely.

6 Electricity

> 6.3 Using conductors and insulators in electrical appliances

We are going to...

- classify materials used in electrical appliances as electrical conductors or insulators
- see how to use electrical appliances safely
- predict whether appliances are being used safely or not
- present results in a dot plot.

Getting started

1. Identify the electrical appliances 1–4.
2. Where in your home do you use most electrical appliances?
3. Do these appliances use the same electricity as the circuit we made in class?

cable	pylon
cord	volt
electric shock	voltage
mains electricity	wall socket
plug	

1

3

2

4

6.3 Using conductors and insulators in electrical appliances

Conductors and insulators and mains electricity

In class you have made circuits with cells with voltages of 1.5 V or 3 V. 'V' stands for **volt**. A volt is a unit to measure the strength of electricity. We describe the strength of a supply of electricity as **voltage**. Cells with a voltage of 1.5 V or 3 V are safe to use.

You may have seen a **pylon** like the one in the photograph. Pylons carry electricity in **cables** (large wires) from where the electricity is made to where it is used in homes, factories and offices. The voltage of electricity carried by these cables is many thousands of volts!

Appliances like microwave ovens, electric kettles and power drills use **mains electricity**. Mains electricity has a much higher voltage than cells. In some countries it is 110 V and in other countries it is over 200 V.

At these high voltages, safety is very important. The parts of an appliance that you touch must be made from insulating material. The parts inside the appliance are made from conducting material so that electricity can pass through.

You know that metals, such as copper, iron and steel, are good electrical conductors. The parts of electrical appliances that let electricity pass through are made of metal. For example, metal is used for the pins in a **plug**. The pins allow electricity to travel from the **wall socket**, through the plug, and into an appliance such as a kettle or television.

When we handle the plug we only touch the cover. This is made of plastic, which is a good insulator.

Remember to never touch a bare electric wire, especially if your fingers are damp or sweaty.

133

6 Electricity

> **Activity 1**
>
> **Classify materials used in electrical appliances as electrical conductors or insulators**
>
> Look at the picture of electric wire.
>
> **Questions**
>
> 1. Why is the wire covered in plastic?
> 2. Why is the wire made of copper?
>
> Find three examples of appliances at home or at school.
>
> 3. Name the appliances.
> 4. What voltage of electricity do these appliances use?
> 5. Choose one of the appliances on your list. Draw a picture of it and label the materials used. Classify the materials as conductors or insulators of electricity.
> 6. Look for electrical appliances at home. List them according to the room they are in. Draw a dot plot to present your results. You can find out how to draw a dot plot at the end of this book.

Electric shocks

If mains electricity flows through your body you will get an **electric shock**. You will be badly burnt, your heart could stop beating and you could die.

Damaged electrical wiring is one of the main causes of accidents with electricity.

Plastic insulation often wears off the copper wires – you can get a shock if you touch the wires.

Never place an electric wire under a carpet. When people walk on the carpet the plastic wears off the copper wires. When bare copper wires touch each other, electricity flows between them and this can start a fire.

Never pull a plug out like this. This damages the **cord** and the wires become bare. If you handle the bare wires you could get an electric shock. Turn off the switch before you pull out the plug. Grip the plug, which is made of insulating plastic, to pull the plug out of the socket.

6.3 Using conductors and insulators in electrical appliances

Be careful not to plug too many electrical devices into the same socket. This can overload the socket and could give you a shock if you touch the socket or one of the plugs. It could also cause a fire.

Activity 2

Predict safe or unsafe use of appliances

1. Predict what could happen to the person in the picture.
2. Copy and complete these sentences to explain why this could happen.

   He is pushing a _____ screwdriver into the holes of the _____ when the power is on. The electricity could flow from the _____ in the wall to the screwdriver in his _____. The wires and screwdriver are made of _____ which is a _____ of electricity.

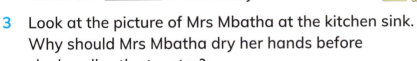

3. Look at the picture of Mrs Mbatha at the kitchen sink. Why should Mrs Mbatha dry her hands before she handles the toaster?

How am I doing?

Explain the difference between a 1.5 V cell and mains electricity to a member of your family.

G Electricity

What did you learn about using electricity safely at home?
Do you think what you learnt today will be useful?

Look what I can do!

☐ I can classify materials used to make electrical appliances as electrical conductors or insulators.

☐ I can understand how insulators help us to use mains electricity safely.

☐ I can make predictions using my knowledge of conductors and insulators.

☐ I can present my results in a dot plot.

6.4 Switches

We are going to...

- describe how a simple switch is used to open and close a circuit
- make a prediction and test our prediction to see if it is correct
- see that an electrical device will not work if there is a break in the circuit
- choose equipment to carry out an investigation and use it appropriately
- identify risks and carry out practical work safely.

Getting started

Look at the picture.

1. What happens when Sofia turns the switch on?
2. What happens when Sofia turns the switch off?

switch

6 Electricity

Putting a switch in a circuit

A **switch** is another component in an electrical circuit. The switch turns the electric current on or off. It is the same idea as turning a tap on or off.

So far you have made circuits with no switch. To break the circuit you broke the wire. A switch lets you turn a lamp on and off when you like, without having to break wires.

Think like a scientist 1

Make a switch

> **You will need:**
> a small block of wood, two drawing pins, a wire, a sharp knife or wire trimming tools, a metal paper clip (not plastic coated), a plastic or wooden chopstick

Put together the parts as shown.
Strip the plastic off the ends of the two pieces of wire.

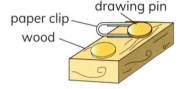

Be careful if using the knife to strip the plastic from the wires. Wait until your teacher is able to help you. You could use wire trimming tools instead.

- Wind one end of each piece of wire to the drawing pins as shown.
- Move the paper clip until it touches the other drawing pin. You should use a wooden or plastic stick (such as a chopstick) to do this. This completes the circuit.
- To switch off, lift the paper clip off the drawing pin. This breaks the circuit.

Questions

1. Why do you use a metal paper clip to make the switch?
2. Why do you use metal drawing pins to make the switch?
3. Why is the base of the switch made of wood?
4. Suggest other suitable materials for making a switch.

6.4 Switches

Think like a scientist 2

Make a circuit with a switch

You will need:
a switch, a cell in a cell holder, a lamp in a lamp holder, 30 cm wire, a sharp knife or wire trimming tools, scissors

- Make a circuit like the one shown.

Remember to follow the safety rules. Wait until your teacher is able to help you if using the knife to strip the plastic from the ends of the wire.

- Predict what will happen when you close the switch.
- Close the switch. Observe the lamp. What happens?
- If the lamp does not light up, check all your connections in the circuit. Try again.

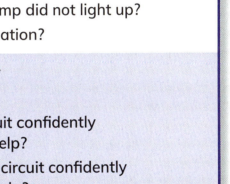

Questions
1. Why does the lamp light up when you close the switch?
2. What must you do with the switch to break the circuit?
3. Draw the circuit you made. Label the cell, the wire, the switch and the lamp.
4. Why did you need to check your connections if the lamp did not light up?
5. Which safety rules did you follow during this investigation?

How am I doing?

- How well did your partner do in the investigation?
- Did your partner connect the components of the circuit confidently on their own, or did they need some help or a lot of help?
- Did your partner use the switch to open or break the circuit confidently on their own, or did they need some help or a lot of help?

Look what I can do!

☐ I can use my knowledge of conductors and insulators to make a simple switch.
☐ I know the risks and work safely doing practical work.
☐ I can make a prediction and test my prediction to see if its correct.
☐ I can see that a lamp will not light up if there is a break in the circuit.

6 Electricity

> 6.5 Changing the number of components in a circuit

We are going to...

- investigate how changing the number or type of components in a circuit make a lamp shine more brightly or less brightly
- identify risks and carry out practical work safely
- make predictions and identify if results support predictions or do not support predictions
- describe simple patterns in results and make a conclusion from results.

Getting started

1. What components have you used so far to build a circuit?
2. Where is the electricity in the circuit?
3. What pushes the electricity around the circuit?
4. What opens and closes the circuit?

battery   brightness
brightly   dimly

Cells and batteries

So far you have mostly made circuits with one cell. Each cell stores 1.5 V of electricity. When we have two or more of these cells connected together we call it a **battery**. The car battery in the picture is 12 V. Your teacher used two cells in the experiment looking at whether water conducted electricity. When the cell or battery is part of a circuit, the stored energy pushes electricity around the circuit. In the next activity you need to use a 3 V battery.

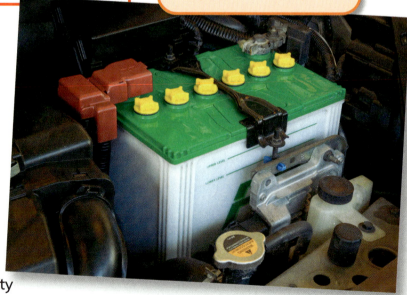

140

6.5 Changing the number of components in a circuit

> **Think like a scientist**
>
> **What happens when we change the number of components in a circuit?**
>
> > **You will need:**
> > three 1.5 V cells in cell holders, three lamps in lamp holders, a switch, wire, a sharp knife or wire trimming tools, scissors, a stick
>
> - Make a table to record your results like this:
>
> | Circuit | Brightness of lamps |
> |---|---|
> | 1 3 V battery, three lamps | |
> | 2 3 V battery, two lamps | |
> | 3 3 V battery, one lamp | |
> | 4 4.5 V battery, three lamps | |
> | 5 3 V battery, three lamps | |
>
> - Make circuit 1 by joining two cells together to make a 3 V battery. Make sure the positive and negative terminals are next to each other.
> - Use the scissors to cut the wire into short lengths. Complete circuit 1 by adding three lamps in lamp holders and a switch.
>
> **Be careful if using the knife to strip the plastic from the wires. Wait until your teacher is able to help you. You could use wire trimming tools instead.**
>
>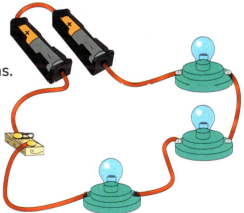
>
> Circuit 1
>
> - Predict what will happen if you close the switch.
> - Close the switch. Observe the lamps.
> - Predict what will happen if you open the switch.
> - Open the switch. Observe the lamps.
> - Make circuit 2 by removing one lamp and a lamp holder so that only two lamps are left in your circuit.
> - Predict what will happen when you close the switch.

6 Electricity

Continued

Remember to follow the safety rules!

- Close the switch. Observe the lamps. Did you notice any difference in the brightness or amount of light from the lamps? Record your result.
- Open the switch.
- Predict what would happen if you remove one more lamp in a lamp holder. This means that only one lamp remains in your circuit (circuit 3). Test your prediction. Record your result.
- Now change the number of cells in your circuit. Make circuit 4 by using three cells and three lamps in lamp holders.
- Close the switch. Observe how brightly the lamps are shining.
- Now open the switch. Decide how you can change this circuit and ask another question about how your change to the circuit will affect the brightness of the lamps. For example, you could remove one of the cells so that there are two cells left (circuit 5). Predict how bright the lamps will be when you close the switch.
- Close the switch. Test your prediction.

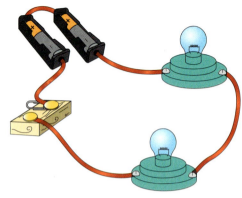

Circuit 2

Questions

1. Identify two risks when doing this investigation.
2. Explain how to stay safe and avoid these risks.
3. Did the lamps shine more **brightly** or more **dimly** when you removed one lamp from the circuit? Why do you think this happened?
4. What happened when you used only one lamp and three cells in the circuit? Why do you think this happened?
5. Did the lamps shine more brightly or more dimly when you removed one cell from the circuit? Why do you think this happened?
6. Identify a pattern in your results. Choose the correct alternatives to complete these sentences:

   The lamps shine **less / more** brightly when you add more lamps to the circuit.

   The lamps shine **less / more** brightly when you add more cells to the circuit.

6.5 Changing the number of components in a circuit

Continued

7 Complete the sentence below to write a conclusion:

Changing the number of _____ or _____ in a circuit can make a lamp _____ or _____.

8 Which type of scientific enquiry did you practise in this investigation?

How am I doing?

How well did your partner do in the investigation?

Was your partner better at connecting the components of the circuit than in the last activity?

How well did your partner add or take away components and re-connect the circuit?

- Confidently on their own?
- Did they need some help?
- Did they need a lot of help?

How well did your partner record results?

Look what I can do!

☐ I can change the number of lamps or cells in a circuit and observe how this affects the brightness of the lamps.

☐ I know the risks and work safely doing practical work.

☐ I can make predictions and see if results support my prediction.

☐ I can identify a pattern in results and make a conclusion.

143

6 Electricity

Project: Batteries

All the circuits you have made included a cell or a battery. These batteries contain chemical substances that react together. This reaction supplies energy. The energy pushes the electricity around the circuit. How did scientists make this discovery?

The Baghdad battery

In June 1936 workers were building a new railway near the city of Baghdad, in present-day Iraq. They found an ancient tomb (a place where a person was buried when they died).

Archaeologists (scientists who study ancient remains) identified things in the tomb to be 2000 years old.

One of the old objects they found in the tomb was a clay jar. The jar had an iron rod coming out of the centre, surrounded by a tube made of copper. Scientists made copies of the object. When they filled the tube with an acid such as vinegar, it produced between 1.5 and 2 volts of electricity between the iron and copper. Archaeologists think that people who lived 2000 years ago could have used batteries like this!

Galvani's discovery

Luigi Galvani was an Italian doctor. In about 1780 he discovered current electricity. He hung a frog's leg on copper hooks over an iron railing. He observed that the frog's leg muscles twitched (moved). Galvani was correct when he said that the twitching was caused by an electrical current. But he thought that the current came from the frog's legs and called it 'animal electricity'.

The voltaic pile

Alessandro Volta was an Italian university professor. He repeated Galvani's experiments many times with different materials. From these experiments he came to the conclusion that it was the two different metals, not the frog's leg, that produced the electricity. The frog's leg showed the presence of the electricity.

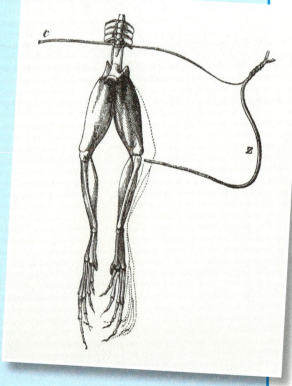

Project: Batteries

Continued

In 1800, after many experiments, he developed his own battery and named it after himself – the 'voltaic pile'.

Continue the story…

Find out more about Alessandro Volta's battery called the voltaic pile. You can use reference books or the internet.

- Describe Volta's battery and how it worked.
- Put your information onto a sheet of paper. Illustrate it with diagrams or pictures.

145

6 Electricity

Check your progress

1 Write **one** word or **two** words to describe each of the following:

   a A device for closing or opening a circuit.

   b A device in a circuit for holding a lamp in place.

   c Something that pushes electricity around a circuit.

2 Which of the following materials are insulators of electricity?

   gold   cork   plastic   aluminium

3 In the circuit alongside:

   a What does the component A do?

   b What must you do to this circuit to turn the lamp off?

   c If you added a second lamp to the circuit, would the lamps glow more brightly or more dimly?

   d If you added another 1.5 V cell to the circuit, would the lamps glow more brightly or more dimly?

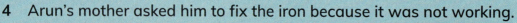

4 Arun's mother asked him to fix the iron because it was not working. Arun got an electric shock!
What had Arun forgotten to do?

Check your progress

> **Continued**
>
> **5** Here are four steps, A to D, that you should take to replace a light lamp safely with a new one.
>
> The steps are in the wrong order. Re-arrange the steps so that they are in the correct order.
>
> A Unscrew the old light lamp.
>
> B Wait for the lamp to cool down.
>
> C Switch the electricity off.
>
> D Screw in the new light lamp.

New science skills

New science skills

Stay safe during practical work

In Stage 4 there are lots of investigations for you to do in groups in the classroom. Here are some general safety rules:

- Make sure the floor areas are clear – don't leave bags and clothes on the floor for people to trip over. Walk, don't run.
- Tie back long hair in case it gets tangled up in your investigation.
- Make sure your clothes can't get caught up in equipment. Wear closed shoes.
- Wear protective clothing when necessary. For example, you may need to wear goggles to protect your eyes. Wear gloves and use tongs when picking up hot things. Your teacher will advise you.
- Handle each piece of equipment with care and put it away carefully when you have finished.
- Be careful with sharp objects such as scissors.
- Never sniff or taste any substances you are working with as they could be harmful.
- Always follow the teacher's instructions. Call your teacher immediately if someone in your group gets hurt.

When building electrical circuits you need to take care to:

- never touch any exposed wires when the circuit is open
- use a wire stripper to cut plastic coating off the ends of wires; this is safer than using a knife.

148

New science skills

Repeating measurements or observations can get more reliable data

Zara and Sofia are investigating how long it takes for different substances to melt. They test frozen water, milk and orange juice. They pour the same amount of each liquid into an ice tray. They put the ice tray in the freezer and wait for the liquid to solidify. They put the ice tray of frozen liquids on the window ledge in the hot Sun.

They use a timer to measure how long it takes each substance to melt.

Reliable data means data that are closest to the true answers. So the girls repeat the test three times. Here are their results:

Time in minutes	Water	Milk	Orange juice
Time taken to melt in test 1	13	11	10
Time taken to melt in test 2	13	11	6
Time taken to melt in test 3	13	12	11

New science skills

The girls got the same result each time for water. The results for milk were almost the same. But the second result for orange juice was much lower than the first and third results. They decided to test orange juice a fourth time. This time the orange juice took 10 minutes to melt. So they decided the second result was wrong. They were able to make this conclusion because they repeated the test.

Repeating observations

Marcus is observing birds in the park. He is collecting data on what foods pigeons and starlings eat.

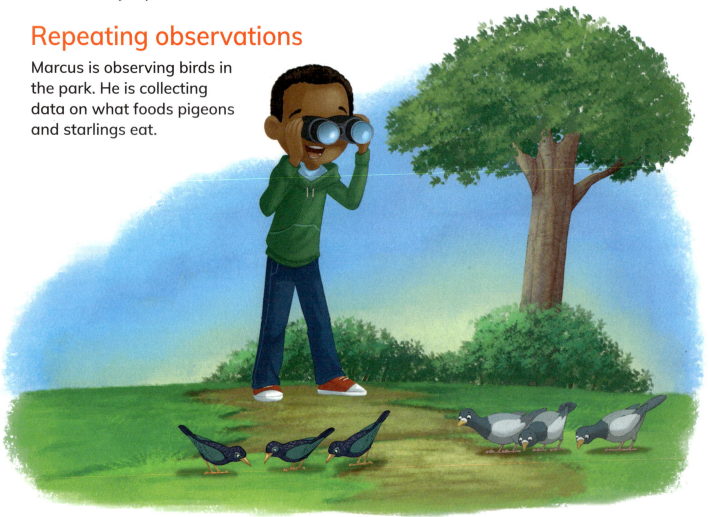

On Monday he observes pigeons and starlings eating seeds. He decides to repeat his observations the following day to see if the birds were eating seeds again or something different.

On Tuesday morning he returns to the park and observes the pigeons eating the leftover crumbs from someone's lunch and he saw a starling eating a grasshopper.

That same afternoon he saw a starling and a pigeon eating a fruit that had fallen off a tree.

If Marcus had written his report on Monday he would have said that pigeons and starlings eat seeds.

After repeating his observations Marcus can report that pigeons and starlings eat a variety of foods such as seeds, bread crumbs and fruit and that starlings also eat grasshoppers. So repeating observations made his data more reliable.

Measuring in standard and non-standard units

We measure things all the time. For example, we measure how much flour we must put in a cake mix and the time it will take the cake to bake in the oven. We also measure things like our height and mass.

We use different units of measurement to measure different things. When we measure our mass, we use kilograms. We use hours to measure the length of a day. In this book, you will use seconds to measure the amount of time it takes a solid to flow through a funnel. Kilograms, hours and seconds are standard units of measurement. In science, we measure using standard units.

Why do we use standard units?

New science skills

Standard units are used all around the world. We use them because they do not change and because other people can understand them. Using standard units allows us to compare our measurements with other people's. Using standard units also makes measuring more accurate, which is important to scientists.

Sometimes people use units of measurements that are non-standard. For example, we measure the amount of sugar we put in our tea in teaspoonfuls, but teaspoons are not all the same size. In the past, people used parts of the human body such as hands, arms, fingers and legs as the units of measurement for length. Long ago, a cubit was the length of the arm from the elbow to the tip of the middle finger. Because arm and hand lengths vary, non-standard measurements like the cubit are not very accurate. People get different results for the same measurement when they use non-standard units. We now measure length in standard units such as millimetres (mm), centimetres (cm) or metres (m). By using standard units everyone gets the same or similar results when they measure the same things.

Using non-standard measurements can make other people confused if they are not using the same units for measuring or do not understand the units you are using.

How to draw a dot plot

A dot plot is a good way to show numbers of something. For example, Arun asks 20 people in his class how many brothers and sisters they have in their families. The numbers they give him are his data.

He records the data like this:

Brothers and sisters	None	One	Two	Three	Four	Five or more
	✓✓	✓✓✓	✓✓✓✓✓	✓✓✓✓	✓✓✓	✓✓

Arun presents his data on a dot plot.

He draws a line with a ruler for the x-axis (the line that goes across the page or horizontal axis). Then he divides the axis into six equal parts. Each part is for one of the groups on his table – none, one, and so on. He labels the parts like this:

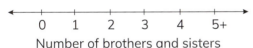

Then he draws dots above each number on the x-axis. Each dot represents a ✓ on his table.

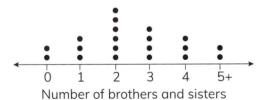

The dot plot clearly shows results such as:

1. Most of the learners have two brothers and sisters.
2. Only two learners have no brothers and sisters or five or more brothers and sisters.

Glossary and index

absorb	to take in a substance. For example, if you spill a liquid you can pat it with a paper towel. The paper towel absorbs the liquid	105
anticlockwise	the opposite of clockwise which is the direction the hands of the clock move	113
apparent movement	the movement does not really happen but it looks like it happens	118
ash	burnt material. For example, the grey powdery material left when wood has burnt	75
asteroid	a rocky mass that orbits the Sun. These are similar to planets but much smaller	110
axis	anything that spins or rotates has to turn around a central line. This line is the axis	113
battery	a source of energy or power for a circuit, made up of more than one cell, which pushes electricity around a circuit	140
beak	the part of a bird used to catch and hold food	88
bones	hard, strong parts inside our body that give our body shape and keep us upright	3
brightly	shines with a stronger light	142
brightness	how strong the light shines	142
cable	a rope of wires	133
carnivore	an animal that eats other animals	43
change of state	when materials and substances change from one form to another when they are heated or cooled	58

chemical reaction	when we mix together two substances and they both change to make a new substance	64
closest	the one that is nearest. For example, The closest shop from my home is just down our road	110
coastal area	a low lying area along the border between land and sea. The coastline is the outline of the border between the land and the sea as you see it on a map	84
comet	a lump of ice and dirt which moves in a large orbit around the Sun. Halley's comet (named after the astronomer Halley) takes 76 years to make one orbit around the Sun	110
compare	to look at two or more things and say what is the same about them and what is different about them	52
composite volcano	a volcano that erupts lava and ash which builds up into a cone-shaped mountain. 'Composite' means being made up of more than one type of material	75
conclusion	what you have found out from an investigation	35
conductor	a material that allows electricity or heat to pass through it	125
consumer	a living thing that cannot make its own food and obtains energy by eating other living things, usually an animal that eats plants or other animals	43
contract	when muscles get shorter and fatter. Muscles feel hard when they contract	10
cord	the plastic-coated wire that connects to a plug at one end and an appliance at the other end	134
core	the centre of the Earth. 'Core' is a commonly used word in English that always means 'at the centre of'. For example, the core of an apple is at the centre of the apple, the core ideas are the ideas most central to the topic	72

155 〉

crack open	to break something open	88
crater	a large hole at the top of a volcano where material erupts	75
crust	the outer layer of the Earth. Note that 'crust' is also used in English to describe the hard outer layer of bread	72
destroy	to make something not exist anymore, for example to destroy a letter by burning it	41
dimly (adverb)	shines with a weaker light	142
distilled water	water that has been boiled and the steam has been allowed to cool down to form liquid water again. Distilled water has no salts dissolved in it and so it is pure water	128
earthquake	a shaking of the Earth	82
electric appliances	machines that need electrical energy to make them work, for example an electric kettle	39
electric shock	the effect of a sudden flow of electricity through a person's body. A person's heart can be badly affected and the person can have a heart attack and die	134
electrical energy	the form of energy we get from electricity	39
energy	anything that can cause movement or carry out an action	32
energy transfer	when energy moves from one place to another place or from one object to another object	35
epicentre	the point on the surface of the Earth immediately above the focus. The epicentre is where the most damage occurs	83
erupt	to shoot out suddenly. For example, if you boil milk in a saucepan and do not watch it, the milk can erupt out of the pan and on to the stove	75

exoskeleton	the hard skins or shells on the outside of the bodies of some invertebrates	17
external structure	materials that make up the surface of the Earth and other things. 'External' means 'outside', so we are referring to materials on the surface of the Earth that we can see	71
fins	small flat organs on a fish's body which help it to swim	88
focus	the point in the crust under the Earth's surface where the earthquake starts; we also use the word 'focus' in English to mean the central point – for example, the focus of the lesson was earthquakes	83
food chain	a drawing that shows the order in which animals eat plants and other animals to get energy	44
frame	something that gives support and shape from the inside	3
function	the job or use of something, for example the function of a pen is to write	6
furthest	the one that is the most far away	111
germs	very tiny living things that can cause diseases, for example we wash our hands before we eat so we don't get germs on our food	26
gills	organs that fish have to allow them to breathe in water	88
globe	a model of the Earth. However, in everyday life you often hear people talking about the globe meaning the whole world	113
herbivore	an animal that eats plants	43

hip	the bone that joins the leg to the upper part of the body	3
identification key	a set of questions that allows us to name or group things	19
image	a picture of the object that you see on a screen or in a mirror	103
infect	when the germs get into your body and make you ill	26
infectious disease	a disease that is caused by germs	26
instructions	information that tells us how to do something, for example Ali has a set of instructions to tell him how to build a model car	23
insulator	a material that does not allow electricity or heat to pass through it	125
internal structure	materials that make up the inside of the Earth. 'Internal' means 'inside' so we are referring to materials inside the Earth that we can't see	71
invertebrate	an animal that has no backbone or spine	17
jaw	the skull bone that moves when we eat or talk	3
landslide	a mass of rocks and soil that slides down a slope. The vibrations from the earthquake cause these to happen	83
lava	magma that reaches the surface of the Earth	75
length	how long something is; for example, the length of a ruler is 30 cm	7
magma	melted rocks	72
mains electricity	high voltage electricity that is sent to homes, schools, factories and offices to provide power for machines, lighting and appliances	133

mantle	the layer of the Earth below the crust which consists of magma	72
materials	kinds of matter that we use, such glass and metal	49
medicines	substances that we use to help us get better when we are ill, for example cough mixture helps us to stop coughing	23
melting	when a solid changes state to become a liquid	58
mirror	a very smooth, shiny surface that reflects light well	103
model	an object or drawing that helps us understand how something works or see what something looks like that we can't see in real life	4
muscles	parts of the body that are joined to bones and allow us to move	6
omnivore	an animal that eats plants and other animals	43
orbit	the movement of a body in space around a larger body in space. For example, the Earth moves around the Sun in an orbit. The Moon moves around the Earth in an orbit	109
organs	parts inside the body that do different jobs	6
particles	very tiny pieces of something	50
physical process	when a substance changes form, e.g. melts, but does not become a new substance	60
plateau	a flat uplifted area of rock. For example, most of India and Africa consists of a plateau	75
plug	a device for connecting an electric wire or cable to an electricity supply	133
pour	to make a liquid or other substance flow out of or into a container	55
powder	a solid with fine grains that have air spaces between them, such as baby powder or flour	56

predator	an animal that kills and eats other animals	43
predict	to say what you think will happen based on what you already know or have observed, for example we can predict that we will burn our hands if we touch a hot stove	33
prevent	to stop, for example a raincoat prevents us from getting wet when it rains	23
prey	an animal that a predator kills and eats	43
producer	a plant that makes its own food using energy from the Sun	42
proof	scientific evidence that something is true	100
property	what a substance or material is like, or the way it behaves	54
protect	keep safe from harm, for example, a jacket will protect you from the cold	6
prove	to find proof that something is true when doing a scientific investigation	100
pure water	water with no salts dissolved in it	128
pylon	the structure that carries cables from the power station where electricity is made (or generated) to cities, towns and villages	133
ray	a line that light travels in. We often talk about the Sun's rays	101
ray diagram	a diagram to show how light travels	101
react	this is when a substance changes when it is mixed with another substance	64
reflect	the action of light bouncing off a surface	98
reflection	when light bounces off a surface	103
relax	when muscles get longer and thinner. Muscles feel soft when they relax	10
rib cage	the bones of the chest	3

risk	the possibility of something happening. For example, if you climb a tree, there's a risk you might fall	78
rust	a reddish-brown powder that forms on some metals	64
secondary cone	a small volcano that erupts on the side of the main volcano	76
skeleton	the bones inside our body that are joined together to form a frame	2
skull	the bones of the head	3
solar system	the Sun and the planets, moons, comets and asteroids which move around it. 'Solar' means of the Sun	110
solidifying	when a liquid changes state to become a solid	59
source	where something comes from	96
spacecraft	a vehicle for travelling in space. For example, a space shuttle is a spacecraft which takes scientists to and from the space centre	109
spin	a verb that means to turn very fast. The best example of this is a spinning top	113
spine	the bones of the back	3
strain	to separate solids from the liquid they are in. For example, you use a strainer in the kitchen to separate solid foods from a liquid	89
substance	a particular type of solid, liquid or gas, for example water	49
support	to hold up something so that it doesn't fall down	6
surface	the top layer of something that is next to the air	103
switch	a device for closing or opening a circuit	138

tilted	at an angle, not vertical or horizontal	113
transfers	to move from one place or thing to another. For example, the energy of an earthquake transfers to waves	83
tsunami	a huge wave which happens when an earthquake starts under the sea	84
vaccinations	injections or other medicines that stop us from getting a disease	24
vent	a hole. For example, buildings have vents built into them to allow air in. The vents are grids with holes in	75
vertebrate	an animal that has a backbone or spine	16
volt	a unit to measure the strength of electricity	133
voltage	the measurement of the power of electricity. Mains electricity has a voltage of 110 V in some countries and 220 V in other countries. Check what it is in your country. This voltage is much higher than the voltage you are using in class for science experiments. Then you are using 1.5 V cells	133
wall socket	a hole in the wall connecting the plug on an appliance with the electric cables in the wall	133
wave	a way in which energy travels. For example earthquakes travel through the Earth's crust in waves	83

Acknowledgements

The authors and publishers acknowledge the following sources of copyright material and are grateful for the permissions granted. While every effort has been made, it has not always been possible to identify the sources of all the material used, or to trace all copyright holders. If any omissions are brought to our notice, we will be happy to include the appropriate acknowledgements on reprinting.

Thanks to the following for permission to reproduce images:

Cover image by Omar Aranda (Beehive Illustration)

Unit 1: Dorling Kindersley ltd/Alamy Stock Photo; JonathanLesage/GI; Rzdeb/GI; Angkhan/GI; Andresr/GI; Chris Nash/GI; Sebastian Kaulitzki/Science Photo Library/GI; Tang Ming Tung/GI; Paul Hurlock/GI; Sarayut/GI; Valentinrussanov/GI; Getty Images; Garymilner/GI; Ithinksky/GI; Benedetta Barbanti/GI; Digital Zoo/GI; GlobalP/GI; Julichka/GI; Nattanan726; Morne De Klerk/GI; Difydave/GI; Arlindo71/GI; GlobalP/GI; Kerkla/GI; Marcouliana/GI; Auscape/Universal Images Group/GI; Antagain/GI; GlobalP/GI; Ithinksky/GI; Nick David/GI; KatarzynaBialasiewicz/GI; FatCamera/GI; Robert Brook/GI; ER Productions Limited/GI; Inga Spence/Alamy; Bill Barksdale/Agstockusa/SPL; Eva-Katalin/GI; Aizar Raldes/GI; Unit 2: Cavan Images/GI; Miguel Navarro/GI; Fotokostic/GI; Adam Foster/GI; Getty Images; Eugenio Marongiu/GI; Jose A.Bernat Bacete/GI; Vgajic/GI; Wavebreakmedia/GI; Jose Luis Pelaez Inc/GI; Olesia Feketa/GI; Don Mason/GI; Kenishirotie/GI; SorenP/GI; Maki Nakamura/GI; Colin Langford/GI; Robert Muckley/GI; Picture by Tambako the Jaguar/GI; Bjdlzx/GI; Unit 3: Donald Verry/GI; Markus Guhl/GI; MediaProduction/GI; Studiocasper/GI; Gjohnstonphoto/GI; Tetra Images/GI; CinemaHopeDesign/GI; Jongho Shin/GI; Jirkaejc/GI; Geargodz/GI; Getty Images; Robert Brook/GI; Maria Marinho/GI; Naturediver/GI; Vidalidali/GI; AlexPro9500/GI; Anton Petrus/GI; Unit 4: Stocktrek/GI; Tim UR/GI; Rosemary Calvert/GI; Ibraman3012/GI; Alain Barbezat/GI; Justinreznick/GI; Shayes17/GI; Fridah/GI; Kampee Patisena/GI; Don Bartletti/Los Angeles Times/GI; Athit Perawongmetha/GI; Joe Raedle/GI; Alvaro Santa Ana/Aton Chile/GI; Haje Jan Kamps/GI; Bogdanhoria/GI; Andreveen/GI; Visivasnc/GI; MikeLane45/GI; Susan Walker/GI; Andrew Jones/GI; Jamcgraw/GI; Mint Images-Art Wolfe/GI; TommL/GI; Getty Images; Sarayuth3390/GI; Westend61/GI; 1001nights/GI; Libor Vaicenbacher/GI; Unit 5: Jethuynh/GI; Sahara Prince/Shutterstock; SKrow/GI; Evgeniy Kirillov/GI; Maria Joao Archer/GI; Keith Brofsky/GI; Fotofrog/GI; Custom Life Science Images/Alamy; Michael I I Spivak/GI; Photovideostock/GI; NASA/JPL; NASA/JPL/Michael Benson/GI; ©NASA/Roger Ressmeyer/Corbis/VCG/GI; Imagenavi/GI; Grafissimo/GI; ClaudioVentrella/GI; Unit 6: CribbVisuals/GI; Jayk7/GI; Heibaihui/GI; Serghei Starus/GI; PKM1/GI; Akova/GI; Monkey Business Images/Shutterstock; Rawpixel/GI; Zenstock/GI; Kiankhoon/GI; ZU_09/GI; Ilbusca/GI; Cavan Images/GI; Wayne Eastep/GI; Yamtono_Sardi/GI; Peter Adams; Planet Observer/GI.

Key: GI= Getty Images.